THE MODERN AMERICAN POSTER

ニューヨーク近代美術館所蔵品による
20世紀アメリカのポスター

by J. Stewart Johnson

主催／京都国立近代美術館　東京国立近代美術館
京都国立近代美術館　1983年10月21日(金)————12月 4 日(日)
東京国立近代美術館　1983年12月14日(水)—1984年 1 月22日(日)

Published by The National Museum of Modern Art, Kyoto, and The Museum of Modern Art, New York
Distributed by New York Graphic Society Books
Little, Brown and Company, Boston

This catalog has been produced to accompany an exhibition of posters from the Graphic Design Collection of The Museum of Modern Art, New York, presented at The National Museum of Modern Art, Kyoto, October 21–December 4, 1983 and The National Museum of Modern Art, Tokyo, December 14, 1983–January 22, 1984
The Exhibition was organized under the auspices of The International Council of The Museum of Modern Art, New York

目次

Contents

あいさつ

　京都と東京，両国立近代美術館は昭和53年に，パリの国立ポスター美術館の協力を得て「ヨーロッパのポスター／その源流から現代まで」と題する展覧会を開催し，18世紀後半から現代にいたるフランスを中心としたヨーロッパのポスター・アートの展開を紹介しました。当時から，同展と対をなすものとしてアメリカのポスター展を企画していましたが，ここにニューヨーク近代美術館の全面的な協力のもとに，同館の厖大なポスター・コレクションから213点を選び，今世紀アメリカのポスター・アートの流れと現状を紹介する展覧会を開催します。

　アメリカのポスターの歴史は，ヨーロッパから絶えず影響と刺激を受けながら独自の表現を獲得していく過程であったと言えるでしょう。第1次世界大戦以前のアメリカの作家たちは，ヨーロッパの美術の潮流に敏感でした。1920年代の保守的な時代ののち，30年代および40年代の若い世代の作家たちは，ヨーロッパからの亡命者たち，殊にバウハウスの亡命者たちがもたらしたアイデアに反応を示しはじめました。また戦後はスイスのグラフィック・デザインの単純で明快なイメージを学びとっています。こうした歴史のうえに，おおらかさ，ユーモアを好む国民性などに支えられてアメリカのポスターは1960年代に至って豊かな開花を見たのでした。当時のアメリカのポスターやグラフィック・デザインはアメリカ国内だけでなく，世界中の人々の注目を集めたと言っても過言ではありません。それらは，正に熱いアメリカン・ドリームの香を世界に伝えるグラフィック・メッセージだったのです。またこの時期にはベトナム戦争に対する，多くの反戦ポスターも生まれています。それらは二つの世界大戦下の愛国ポスターと好対照をなしており，興味深いものがあります。

　70年代以降，アメリカのポスターには，それ以前のような熱気が失われたようにも見えます。外見上は静かで落ち着いた感を受けますが，しかし，そのなかでは多様な様式的な試みや，新しい理念の模索が着実に行われていることを忘れてはなりません。

　本展はアメリカのポスターの展開やわが国への影響を示すだけでなく，それを生んだ社会や時代性をも窺うための絶好の機会にもなると信じます。

　本展開催にあたり，その構成等並々ならぬ尽力を賜ったニューヨーク近代美術館建築・デザイン部のＪ.ステュアート・ジョンソン氏をはじめ同部スタッフ，および同館国際評議会に対し，深く感謝の意を表します。

　昭和58年10月

京都国立近代美術館長　河北倫明
東京国立近代美術館長　安達健二

Foreword

In 1978 The National Museum of Modern Art, Kyoto and Tokyo, held an exhibition "The European Poster — from its origin to the present" that showed European work (most of which was from France) from the late 18th century onwards, through the cooperation of the Musée de l'Affiche in Paris. Now, in a related move, an exhibition of American posters has been arranged. The Museum of Modern Art in New York has lent us 213 modern American posters from its vast collection.

The American poster has developed a style of its own under the constant influence and impetus of Europe. American artists before World War I were keenly aware of European art currents. After a conservative period in 1920s, a rising generation of young artists in the '30s and '40s began to respond to the graphic ideas brought by European refugees, particularly those from the Bauhaus. After the War, the clean uncluttered imagery of Swiss artists began to register. Out of all this American poster art flourished anew. In addition, a relaxed broad humor — characteristic of Americans — entered the picture. And American commercial art began to set the pace. These graphic messages created a widespread sense of the American dream. At the same time sentiment against the Vietnam War stirred up another sort of poster art that contrasted acutely with earlier patriotic placards.

Since the '70s that high tide seems to have ebbed somewhat. Nevertheless, we should not be put off by the seeming serenity; underneath we can still feel the seething of fresh ideas and new combinations.

This exhibition provides an opportunity to study the development of the American poster as an art form and its influence upon its Japanese counterpart, as well as offering us some insight into the society and times out of which the work has sprung.

We wish to express our deepest gratitude to Mr J. Stewart Johnson, Curator of Design, at the Museum of Modern Art in New York, and his staff, as well as to the International Council of the Museum, who put so much kind effort into organizing the exhibition.

October 1983

Michiaki Kawakita
Director
The National Museum of Modern Art, Kyoto
Kenji Adachi
Director
The National Museum of Modern Art, Tokyo

近代アメリカのポスター

近代のポスターは目に見えるメッセージであり，見る者に即座に消しがたい印象を与えるよう意図された，文字化された言葉と図化されたイメージ（抽象，具象共に）との結合物である。それはテキストを図解する絵でもなければ，絵を説明するテキストでもなく，この二つの要素を一つの強烈な存在に融合したものである。それは重層した意味を含み，繰り返し吟味する価値のあるものかも知れないが，その第一印象は即時のものでなければならない。つまり，走ったり，歩いたり，車やバスや電車での通りすがりにも目につくものでなければならない。他の多くの芸術表現と同様，ポスターもそれ自体鑑賞して愉しむものであると同時に，見た人をある特定の行動，例えば，劇場へ行く，何らかの政治的または社会的姿勢をとる，製品を買うといったような行動に赴かせる意図をもっている。

19世紀末まで，ポスターは普通印刷屋によって作られた。彼等はさまざまな大きさの活字を組み合わせ，時には，その文字を装飾的な縁飾りの模様で囲んだり，見る人の注意を引くために，様式化したシンボル（例えば，差している指）や小さな飾り模様を補足したりした。色刷石版の発達と，日本の版画にみられる要約して極端にパターン化された非対称的なデザインへの関心とその高まりにより，シェレ，トゥールーズ・ロートレック，ボナールといった画家たちは，活字を放棄したり手描き文字と注意を引く図柄とを組み合わせたりしながら，ポスターの実験をはじめた。1890年代中頃までには，これらの新しいポスターは，すでに広く行われていた。展覧会が開かれ，画商はこれらのポスターを蒐集し，その価値が絵入り本や雑誌で議論された。

これらの出版物が大西洋を渡ることにより，アメリカの作家たちは新しいポスター・アートを自らの目で見ることが出来るようになった。彼等はただちに，自分たちのデザインでそれに反応を示したが，その多くはヨーロッパのポスターの亜流であり，ヨーロッパ的アイディアの引きうつしであるこ

とが多かった。しかし，ウィル・ブラッドレー，エドワード・ペンフィールド，マックスフィールド・パリッシュなどによる最もすぐれた作品はアメリカ国内に眼の肥えた鑑賞者を得たばかりでなく，ヨーロッパの批評家やコレクターによって称讃されるほど質の高いものであった。

第一次世界大戦（1914〜1918）は，あらゆる種類の宣伝ポスターの厖大な需要をもたらした。それはこの新しく抬頭してきた美術を育成するよい機会でもあったのだが，実際にはどちらかと言えば逆戻りであった。それはアメリカにおける戦争ポスターの大部分がグラフィック・デザイナーに依頼されず，雑誌や本の挿絵画家に依頼されたからであった。与えられたテーマをポスターに作ってゆく彼等の方法が，多かれ少なかれそのテキストに添って主題と関連のある図に仕上げることであったとしても驚くにあたらない。これらのポスターは概して，技法的にはリアリスティックであり，内容的にはセンチメンタルに描かれていた。迫真力と視覚的衝撃力を持つポスターとして目立つものはごく少数に過ぎない。

終戦とともにポスターの需要は激減し，作家たちの多くはもとの挿絵画家としての仕事に戻っていった。しかし，すでにアメリカの広告美術，殊にアメリカのポスターは，テキストと絵という保守的な鋳型にしっかりと嵌め込まれていた。1920年代を通じて，ヨーロッパのポスターには当時の最も前衛的な美術運動の影響が著しいにもかかわらず，アメリカのポスターは硬直した島国的状況に置かれたままであった。

こうした状況は，1930年代にヨーロッパの経済的，政治的動乱を逃れて，芸術家や知識人たちがアメリカに安住の地を求めて渡ってこなければ，そのまま続いていたかも知れなかった。1941年，アメリカは第二次世界大戦に参戦するが，その頃までにヨーロッパの最も尖鋭的なすぐれたグラフィック・アーティストの多くが大西洋を渡ってきていた。即ち，ハーバート・バイヤー，ラズロ・モホリ＝ナギ，ハーバート・マター，ジョーゼフ・ビンダー，リオ・リオーニ，A. M. カ

ッサンドラ，ジョン・カルル，E.ミックナイト・カウファーのようなデザイナーたちである。彼等のうち幾人かは，洗練された現代的なイメージで読者を引きつけようと懸命の《ヴォーグ》《ハーパーズ・バザー》《フォーチュン》などの雑誌に仕事を見つけ，また或る者は大きな広告代理店からポスターや高速道路の広告掲示板（当時流行の屋外広告の形式であった）にデザインする依頼を取りつけようとした。殊にナチスが1933年に閉鎖する以前に，ドイツのバウハウスに関係していた人々は，彼等と共にアメリカにもたらしたバウハウスの理論と信條をアメリカの若い世代の人々に教えはじめた。

　第二次世界大戦は，再び大量のポスターを産出し，再びその大部分がグラフィック・アーティストによらず挿絵画家によって制作された。しかし，今度は前大戦時よりも状況は異なっていた。愛国的な激励の言葉を添えた紋切型の絵によるポスターとともに，アメリカ国旗の強く心に訴えるシンボルに基づくポスターや，敵の残忍な風刺画を用いたポスターなど強烈な図による提示が時おり現れた。

　第二次世界大戦直後に属するアメリカのグラフィック・デザイナーたちは，ヨーロッパの巨匠たちの仕事の真只中に曝されたばかりでなく，雑誌《グラフィス》のページを通して当時芽生えを示しはじめていたスイスのグラフィック・デザインにも直面した。《グラフィス》は1944年，スイスで刊行をはじめた雑誌で，規模は国際的であったが，その記事や挿図の多くは専らスイス作品の最近の目ざましい発展ぶりを示すものばかりであった。スイスのポスターはすっきりとした構図，直截なイメージ，空間を構成し主要なメッセージを強調するための簡明な色使い，などに特色があった。その明快さと率直さがアメリカのデザイナーたちに強く訴え，彼等はそれらに匹敵するような作品を制作しはじめた。

　1940年代末及び1950年代の数多くのアメリカのポスターが行なった明快に図化された主張に，あらたに愛想のよいユー

モアが加わった。それは大らかで楽天的でいかにもアメリカ的な特質を示しており，その特質は以後のポスターにしばしば登場してくる。ロバート・ゲージのレヴィーのパンのための一連のポスター（のちにこのうちの一点はハーヴ・ブラウン展の予告の背景に用いられている），ソール・バースの切り紙細工による人物と児童画のようなドローイング，ルイス・ダンズィガーの絵筆に似せたアメリカ国旗，チャーマイエフとガイズマーのペン先に似せたアメリカ国旗，ブランドウィーンとマーコウィッツによるアクワダクト競馬場（ニューヨークっ子にはビッグ A として知られている）での競馬を予告する手綱を引き締められた馬の顔，ポール・ランドの IBM のための判じ絵など。これらはすべて，思わずつりこまれるようなイメージに，ちょっとしたウィットを加えることによって一層引立つものになっている。こうした方法の初期の例は，雑誌《ライフ》の宣伝のためにデニス・ウイーラーが制作したこの雑誌の赤と白の鮮やかなロゴタイプのおどけた解釈に見ることができる。

　60年代のサイケデリック・ポスターにおいてもユーモアは重要な要素であった。それらは若く，反逆的な，麻薬に馴染んだ受け手を狙ったものではあったが，その衝撃は根本的に異っていた。この年代以前のハード・エッジ的な解り易いイメージのポスターにとって替わったこれらのポスターは，狂ったような故意に混乱させた構図を持ち，伝達しようとする内容は渦巻く曲線や不調和な色の網の目の中で，ほとんど判読出来ないまでに偽装されていた。ポスターはまるで一般の人々を閉め出して，奥義を伝受された者だけに理解されるパズルとなってしまった。そのユーモアは嘲笑的で辛辣味を帯び，そのメッセージの精髄は，テッド・シェインのポスター〈ターン・オン，チューン・イン，ドロップ・アウト〉に要約されている。サイケデリック・ポスターは難解であると同時に絢爛としており，国外のグラフィック・デザイナーにすみやかに影響を及ぼしていった。殊に日本では，横尾忠則などのようなデザイナーがこのニュー・マニーリスムスから多く

THE MODERN AMERICAN POSTER

を採用した。

　一見享楽的ではあったが，これらサイケデリック・ポスターは既成の秩序への根深い不信，アメリカにおける市民権闘争や，傷ましいベトナム戦争への介入によって促された抗議ポスターの氾濫によって明白になった，疎隔感を表白するものであった。ベトナム戦争中のアメリカのポスターは，官製でもなくメッセージも愛国的なものではなかった。今回は戦争そのものが敵なのであった。

　1960年代の感情的激しさは，1970年代には燃えつきてしまったようである。グラフィック・デザイナーは内容よりも表現形式により多くの関心を寄せるようになった。芸術の他の分野，殊に建築や絵画と同様，ポスターの分野でも何ら顕著な動きは現われず，アメリカのグラフィック・デザイナーたちが賛同できるような特別な方法も現われなかった。それは多様な時代でもあった。ある者は過去のスタイルを再生し，またある者は新しいアイデアを発展させる方向へ進むべく模索していた。

　この折衷主義はアメリカのポスターに雑多な様式をもたらしつつ80年代までつづいている。将来の方向を予測することは不可能である。ただ一つだけ確実なことは，近代ポスター確立のための長い闘いは，ずっと以前に勝利をおさめていたということである。20世紀初頭の間違った出発，両世界大戦間のイラストレーション全盛を経て，1950年代に決定的な転換がもたらされたのである。来年の，或は以後10年間のアメリカのポスターがどのようなものであれ，そのデザインは統合され，そのメッセージは言葉とイメージの融合を通して伝達されるであろうことを我々は確信することができるのである。

The modern poster is a visual message, an amalgam of written word and graphic image (either abstract or pictorial) that is intended to create an instant indelible impression on the viewer. It is not a case of picture illustrating text nor of text explaining picture, but a fusion of the two elements into a single, striking entity. Although it may contain layers of meaning and repay long and repeated scrutiny, its principal impact must be immediate. It is meant to be caught on the run, by pedestrian or passerby in automobile, bus, or train. Like most other artistic expressions, it can be enjoyed for its own sake, but is also usually intended to provoke the viewer into a specific course of action: to go to the theater, to take some political or social stance, to buy a product.

Until the end of the nineteenth century, posters were generally composed by printers, who put together arrangements of type in a variety of weights and sizes and sometimes supplemented their texts with decorative borders, conventionalized symbols (a pointing finger, for example), or vignettes to help catch the viewer's attention. With the development of color lithography, however, and with the upsurge of interest in the spare, strongly patterned, asymmetrical graphic designs found in Japanese prints, artists such as Cheret, Toulouse-Lautrec, and Bonnard began to experiment with posters, abandoning type and weaving together hand lettering and evocative images. By the mid-1890s, the popularity of these new posters had become widespread: exhibitions were held, connoisseurs collected them, and their virtues were discussed in illustrated books and magazines.

These publications, traveling across the Atlantic, made it possible for American artists to see the new poster art for themselves, and they quickly responded with designs of their own. Many were derivative; occasionally they were blatant copies of European ideas. But the best —the work of designers like Will Bradley, Edward Penfield, and Maxfield Parrish—were of sufficient quality not only to find an appreciative audience at home but to be acclaimed by European critics and collectors.

The 1914-18 World War, which resulted in a huge

demand for propaganda posters of all sorts, might have been expected to further this emerging art; but if anything it set it back. This is because the great majority of commissions for war posters in the United States went not to graphic designers but to magazine and book illustrators. Their approach when given a subject to turn into a poster, not surprisingly, was to produce a more or less relevant illustration to accompany the text. These tended to be prettily drawn, realistic in technique, and sentimental in concept. Only a few stand out as having any real power or visual punch.

At the end of the war, much of the market for posters dried up and most of the artists returned to their primary pursuits as illustrators. By now, however, American advertising art in general and American posters in particular had become firmly set in a conservative mold of text and picture. Throughout the 1920s, when the most avant-garde art movements were reflected in European posters, American poster art remained rigidly insular.

This situation might have gone on indefinitely had it not been for the influx of artists and intellectuals who sought refuge in America in the 1930s as they fled the economic and political turmoil of Europe. By the time the United States entered World War II in 1941, many of Europe's most advanced and accomplished graphic artists had crossed the Atlantic—designers of the caliber of Herbert Bayer, László Moholy-Nagy, Herbert Matter, Joseph Binder, Leo Lionni, A. M. Cassandre, Jean Carlu, and E. McKnight Kauffer. Some found work with magazines such an *Vogue, Harper's Bazaar,* and *Fortune,* which were anxious to project a sophisticated contemporary image to their readers. Some managed to get commissions from the powerful advertising agencies to design posters or highway billboards (the prevalent form of outdoor advertising at this time). And some—especially those who had been associated with the Bauhaus in Germany before the Nazis closed it down in 1933—began to teach, communicating the theories and convictions they brought with them to a younger generation of Americans.

World War II once again generated a great number of posters, and once again the majority were produced by illustrators rather than by graphic artists. This time, however, there was more variety. Along with the many posters made up of conventionally drawn pictures appended to patriotic exhortations, occasional strong graphic statements appeared, some built on the poignant symbol of the American flag, some employing savage caricatures of the enemy.

The generation of graphic designers that came of age in the United States just after World War II was exposed not only to the work of the European masters in its midst but to Swiss graphic design, which was burgeoning at the time, through the pages of *Graphis* magazine. Although *Graphis,* which had begun publication in 1944 in Switzerland, was international in scope, many of its articles and illustrations were devoted to the latest developments in Swiss work. Swiss posters were characterized by clean, uncluttered compositions; striking, easily grasped images; and an uncomplicated use of color that helped organize space and lend emphasis to the essential message. Their clarity and directness strongly appealed to American designers, who began to turn out comparable work.

In addition to the decisive graphic statements made by many American posters of the late 1940s and '50s, an ingratiating humor surfaced. Easy, broad, it was peculiarly American in character and has cropped up again and again since. Robert Gage's series of posters for Levy's bread (one of which subsequently was expropriated as the background for an announcement of an exhibition by the artist Herb Brown); Saul Bass's paper-cutout figures and childlike drawings; Louis Danziger's American-flag paintbrush and Chermayeff and Geismar's American-flag pen nib; Brandwein and Markowitz's straining horse's head advertising a racing meet at the Aquaduct racetrack (known simply as the "Big A" to New Yorkers); and Paul Rand's recent rebus for IBM: all gain by adding a fillip of wit to compelling images. Perhaps the prime example of this approach is the campaign publicizing *Life* with Dennis

Wheeler's playful interpretations of the magazine's distinctive red and white logo.

Humor was also an important element of the psychedelic posters of the '60s. Aimed as they were, however, at a young, rebellious, drug-oriented audience, their impact was radically different. The hard-edged, immediately comprehensible images of the earlier posters were superseded by frenzied, purposely confusing compositions in which messages were disguised to the point of near-incomprehensibility within webs of swirling lines and jarring colors. Posters became puzzles to be understood by the initiated, excluding everyone else. Their humor tended to be mocking, abrasive; their quintessential message was summed up in Ted Shaine's poster "Turn On, Tune In, Drop Out." Psychedelic posters were as brilliant as they were enigmatic and had an immediate influence on graphic design outside America, particularly in Japan, where designers such as Tadanori Yokoo adopted many of the new mannerisms.

Although ostensibly hedonistic, psychedelic posters suggested a deep distrust of the established order, a sense of alienation that became explicit in the rash of protest posters prompted by the civil rights struggle in the United States and, most painfully, by America's involvement in the Vietnam war. During *this* war, American posters were not sponsored by the government, nor were their messages piously patriotic. This time the war itself was the enemy.

The emotional intensity of the 1960s seemed to burn itself out in the '70s. Graphic designers became more concerned with form, less with content. As with the other arts, particularly architecture and painting, no dominant movement emerged, no particular approach to which American graphic designers generally could subscribe. It was a time of diversity. Some designers revived past styles, others sought to work their way towards developing new ideas.

This eclecticism has continued into the '80s, with American posters taking motley forms. It is impossible to predict their future direction. One thing is certain though: the old battle for the modern poster has long since been won. After the false start at the turn of the century and the ascendency of illustration from World War I through World War II, during the '50s there was a decisive turnaround. Whatever American posters may look like next year or next decade, we can feel certain their designs will be integrated, their messages conveyed through a melding of word and image.

図版
Plates

1
作者不明
ウォルター L・メイン　三つのリング・ショー　1900年頃

Unknown
Walter L. Main　3 Ring Shows　c. 1900

2
ウィル・ブラッドレー
チャップブック　1895

Will Bradley
The Chap Book　1895

3
ウィル・ブラッドレー
ホワイティングの標準紙　1900年頃

Will Bradley
Whiting's Standard Papers　c. 1900

4
ウィル・ブラッドレー
チャップブック　5月号　1895

Will Bradley
The Chap Book　May　1895

7
ウィル・ブラッドレー
ウィル・ブラッドレーの本　1896

Will Bradley
Bradley　His Book　1896

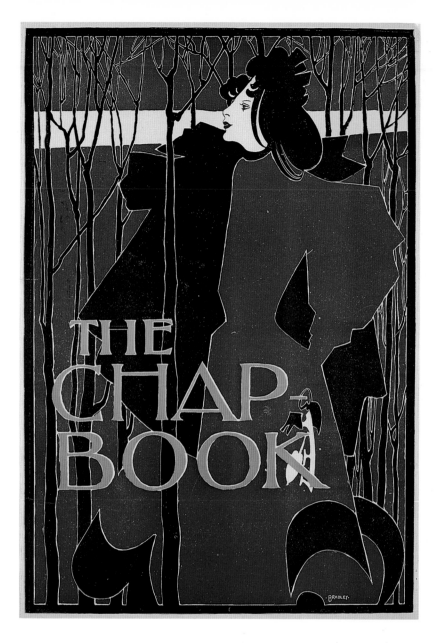

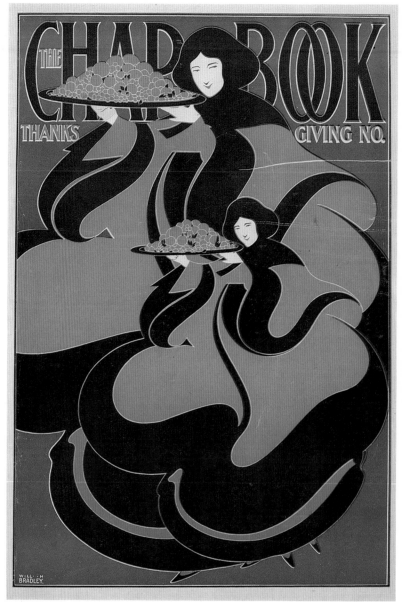

5
ウィル・ブラッドレー
チャップブック　1895

Will Bradley
The Chap Book　1895

6
ウィル・ブラッドレー
チャップブック　感謝祭号　1895

Will Bradley
The Chap Book　Thanksgiving No.　1895

8
作者不明
ヴィクター自転車　1898年頃

Unknown
Victor Cycles　c. 1898

9
エドワード・ペンフィールド
ハーパーズ　3月号　1897

Edward Penfield
Harper's　March　1897

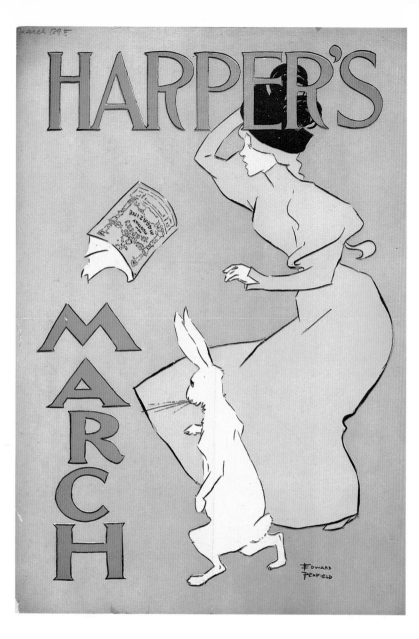

10
エドワード・ペンフィールド
ハーパーズ　3月号　1895

Edward Penfield
Harper's　March　1895

11
エドワード・ペンフィールド
ハーパーズ　7月号　1894

Edward Penfield
Harper's,　July　1894

12
エドワード・ペンフィールド
ハーパーズ　8月号　1896

Edward Penfield
Harper's　August　1896

13
ウィリアム L. カークヴィル
リッピンカッツ　8月号　1895

William L. Carqueville
Lippincott's　August　1895

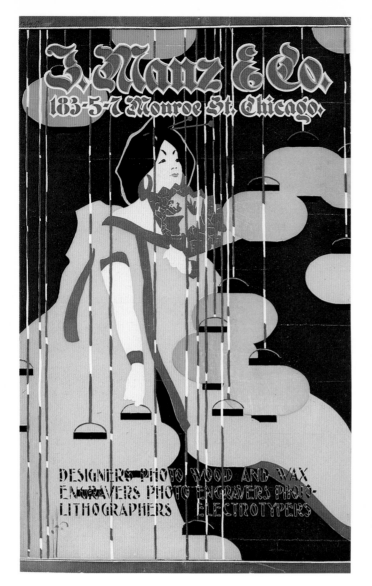

14
作者不明
J. マンツ・アンド・カンパニー　1896年頃

Unknown
J. Manz & Co.　c. 1896

15
チャールズ・ハーバート・ウッドベリー
センチュリー　7月号　1895

Charles Herbert Woodbury
The July Century　1895

16
ウィリアム・サージャント・ケンドール
スクリブナーズ1月号にロバート・ブラム描く大装飾画　1900年頃

William Sargent Kendall
Robert Blum's Great Decorative Paintings in January Scribner's　　c. 1900

17
マックスフィールド・パリッシュ
スクリブナーズ　1897

Maxfield Parrish
Scribner's　1897

18
ジュールス・グラン
スクリブナーズ　セントルイス博覧会号　1904

Jules Guran
Scribner's　St. Louis Exposition　1904

19
作者不明
勝利のために公債を　1917年頃

Unknown
V Invest　c. 1917

20
J. アレン・セント・ジョン
ドイツ野郎の痕跡を消し去れ　1917

J. Allen St. John
The Hun　His Mark　Blot It Out　1917

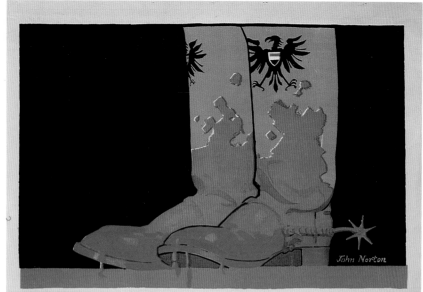

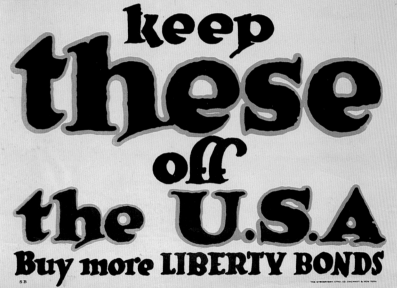

21
ジョン・ウォーナー・ノートン
奴らをアメリカに寄せつけるな 1918

John Warner Norton
Keep These Off the U. S. A. 1918

22
エルスウォース・ヤング
ベルギーを忘れるな 1918

Ellsworth Young
Remember Belgium 1918

24
ジェイムズ・モントゴメリー・フラッグ
合衆国陸軍へ来れ！ 1917

James Montgomery Flagg
I Want You for the U. S. Army 1917

25
ジェイムズ・モントゴメリー・フラッグ
めざめよ　アメリカ・デー 1917

James Montgomery Flagg
Wake Up America Day 1917

26
ルイス・ファンチャー
合衆国公式戦争写真　1917

Louis Fancher
U. S. Official War Pictures　1917

29
フレデリック・ジョージ・クーパー
イギリスへのアメリカの贈物　1918

Frederick George Cooper
America's Tribute to Britain　1918

23
ジョセフ・ペネル
この自由は滅びない　1917年頃

Joseph Pennell
That Liberty Shall Not Perish　c. 1917

27
L. N. ブリットン
もっと食べよ　節食せよ　1917年頃

L. N. Britton
Eat More　Eat Less　c. 1917

28
コールズ・フィリップス
明りが石炭を食う　1917年頃

Coles Phillips
Light Consumes Coal　c. 1917

31
ユージン・ガイズ
ナジモヴァ〈サロメ〉 1922

Eugene Gise
Nazimova Salome 1922

32
ユージン・ガイズ
ナジモヴァ〈サロメ〉　1922

Eugene Gise
Nazimova　Salome　1922

33

30
アーノルド・ゲンスィ
点呼（演劇ポスター）　1918

Arnold Genthe
The Roll Call　1918

33
ブルベーカー
グッド・ブック　1927年頃

Brubaker
A Good Book　c. 1927

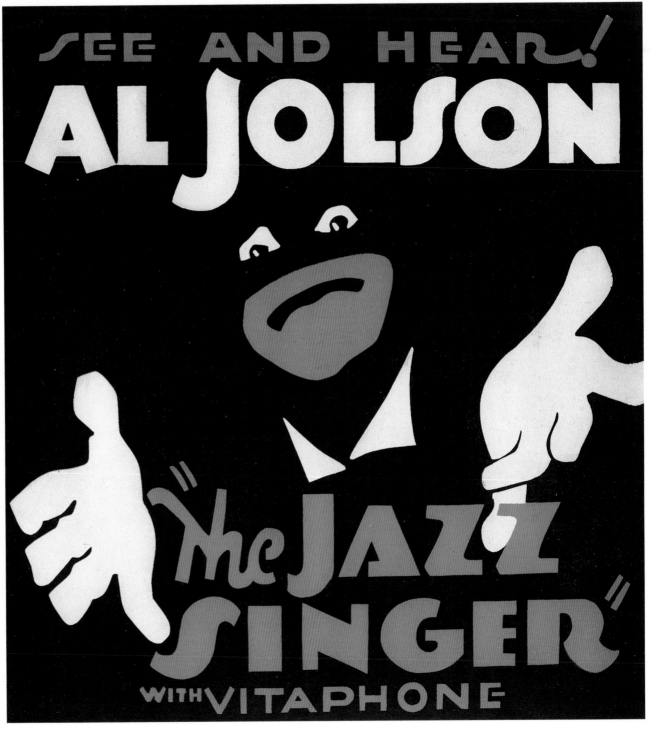

34
ウィリアム・オールバック＝リヴィ
アル・ジョルスン〈ジャズ・シンガー〉　1927

William Auerbach-Levy
Al Jolson "The Jazz Singer" 1927

-KEEPS LONDON GOING

35
マン・レイ
地下鉄がロンドンを動かす　1932

Man Ray
Keeps London Going　1932

36
オーティス・シェパード
リグレイのスペアミント・ガム　1936

Otis Shepherd
Wrigley's Spearmint Gum　1936

A. M. カッサンドラ
ご覧，フォードが通るよ　1937

A. M. Cassandre
Watch the Fords Go By　1937

38
レスター・ビヨー
水道を（農務省農村電化促進局）　1937

Lester Beall
Running Water　1937

39
レスター・ビヨー
ラジオを（農務省農村電化促進局）　1937

Lester Beall
Radio　1937

40
レスター・ビヨー
農作業の機械化を（農務省農村電化促進局）　1937

Lester Beall
Farm Work　1937

41
レスター・ビヨー
電灯を（農務省農村電化促進局）　1937

Lester Beall
Light　1937

42
ジョーゼフ・ビンダー
一番大切な車輪　1951

Joseph Binder
The Most Important Wheels　1951

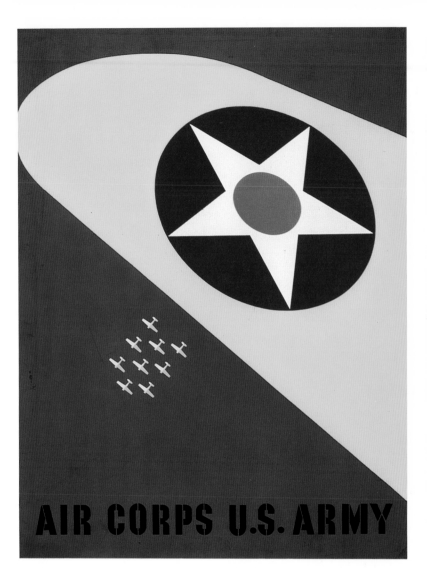

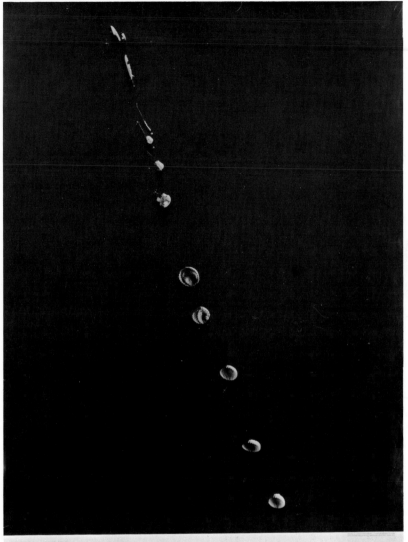

43
ジョーゼフ・ビンダー
合衆国陸軍航空隊　1941

Joseph Binder
Air Corps U. S. Army　1941

44
作者不明
降下海兵隊　1941

Unknown
Paramarines　1941

41

45
ジョン・カルル
アメリカの回答！ 生産 1942

Jean Carlu
America's Answer! Production 1942

46
ジョン・カルル
彼等に銃身を　1941

Jean Carlu
Give 'em Both Barrels　1941

43

47
ヘンリー・カーナー
使った食用油を蓄えよう 1943

Henry Koerner
Save Waste Fats 1943

49
作者不明
増産を 1942年頃

Unknown
More Production 1942

48

チャールズ・コイナー
ベストを尽くせ 1941

Charles Coiner
Give It Your Best! 1942

45

50
リオ・リオーニ
前進！ 1941

Leo Lionni
Keep 'em Rolling！ 1941

51
リオ・リオーニ
前進！ 1941

Leo Lionni
Keep 'em Rolling！ 1941

52
ハーバート・マター
アメリカが呼んでいる　1941

Herbert Matter
America Calling　1941

53
ジョン A. ゲイドス
米大陸には敵を寄せつけない　1942

John A. Gaydos
En Las Americas　1942

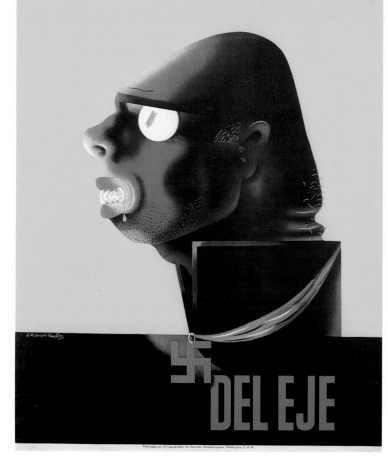

54
E. ミックナイト・カウファー
枢軸側の新秩序とは… 1942

E. McKnight Kauffer
El Nuevo Orden 1942

55
カール・カーラー
ヴィクター・アンコナ
これが敵だ 1942

Karl Koehler
Victor Ancona
This Is the Enemy 1942

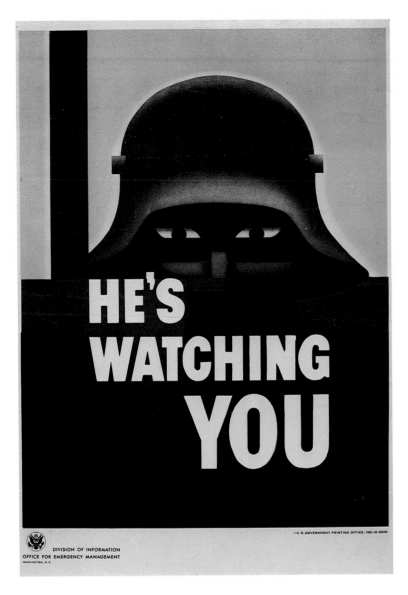

56
グレン・グロー
奴があなたを見張っている　1942

Glenn Grohe
He's Watching You　1942

57
スティヴン・ドハノス
不用心なお喋りの報い　1944

Stevan Dohanos
Award for Careless Talk　1944

58
ヘンリー・カーナー
誰かが喋った　1943年頃

Henry Koerner
Someone Talked　c. 1943

a careless word

...another cross

59
ジョン・アサートン
不用意なひと言が墓標をふやす　1943

John Atherton
A Careless Word　Another Cross　1943

60
ジーン・カルル
地下鉄広告で販売促進を　1947

Jean Carlu
Stop 'em to Sell 'em　1947

61
エリック・ニッチ
迅速，反復，あざやかに　1947

Erik Nitsche
Say It Fast　Often　in Color　1947

62
ポール・ランド
地下鉄ポスターはうける　1947

Paul Rand
Subway Posters Score　1947

53

63
ポール・ランド
インターフェイス・デー　1951

Paul Rand
Interfaith Day　1951

64
ポール・ランド
インターフェイス・デー　1954

Paul Rand
Interfaith Day　1954

65
ベン・シャーン
反動の支配を打ち破れ　1944

Ben Shahn
Break Reaction's Grip　1944

66
レスター・ビヨー
スラム街が犯罪の温床となる　1941

Lester Beall
Slums Breed Crime　1941

67
ミルトン・エィコフ
差別を無くそう　1949

Milton Ackoff
Wipe out Discrimination　1949

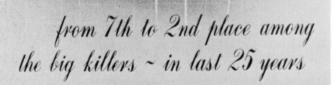

68
フェルネイゴォ
癌の増加　1947年頃

Fellnagel
Cancer　c. 1947

69
カーサコヴ
確かめよ　梅毒防止のために血液検査を受けよう　1947年頃

Karsakov
Know for Sure　Get a Blood Test for Syphilis　c. 1947

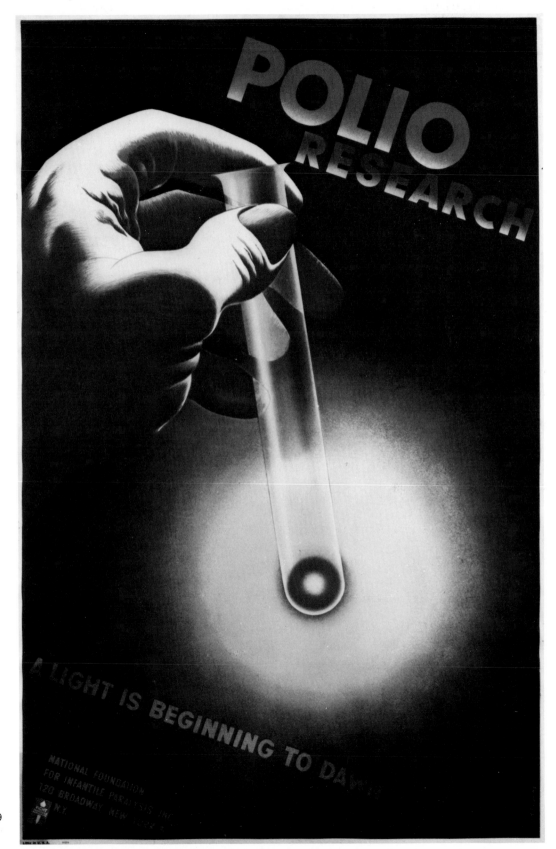

70
ハーバート・バイヤー
小児麻痺研究　1949

Herbert Bayer
Polio Research　1949

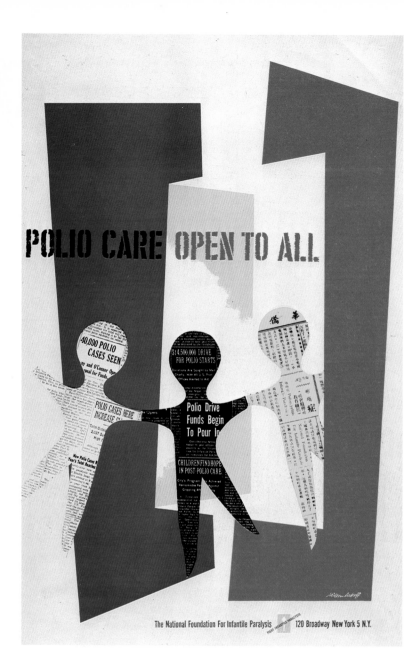

71
ミルトン・エィコフ
小児麻痺の治療を皆んなに 1949

Milton Ackoff
Polio Care Open to All 1949

72
ハーバート・マター
この子等のうちの一人は小児麻痺に罹った 1950

Herbert Matter
One of Them Had Polio 1950

73
ロバート・ゲージ
レヴィーズ　ニューヨークが平らげている！　1952

Robert Gage
Levy's　New York Is Eating It Up！　1952

75
ハーブ・ブラウン
ハーブ・ブラウン個展ポスター　1965

Herb Brown
Herb Brown　1965

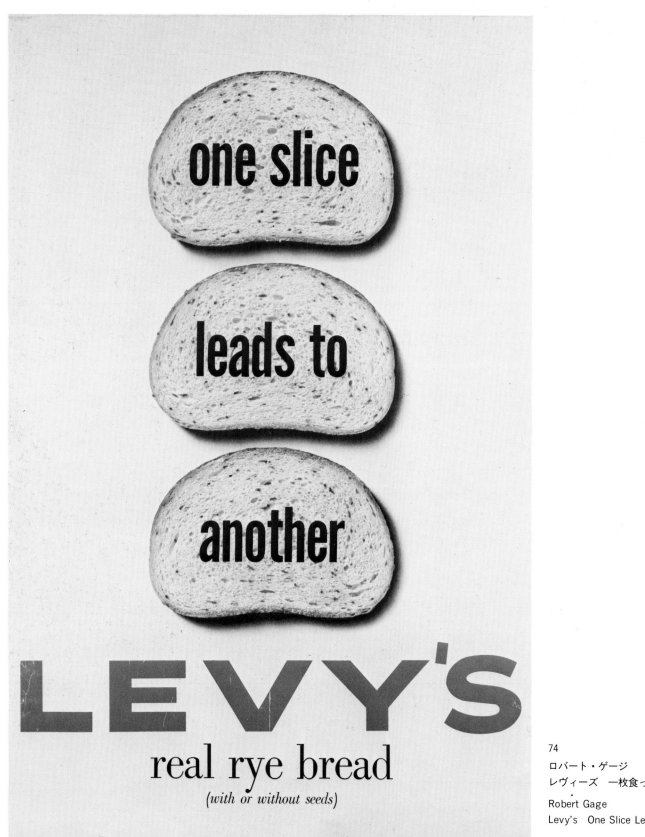

74
ロバート・ゲージ
レヴィーズ　一枚食ってはまた一枚　1952
Robert Gage
Levy's　One Slice Leads to Another　1952

77

マイケル・エングルマン

お早ようはインクワイアラーから　1958

Michael Engelmann
Good Mornings Begin with The Inquirer　1958

78

マイケル・エングルマン

お早ようはインクワイアラーから　1958

Michael Engelmann
Good Mornings　Begin with The Inquirer　1958

SINGLE PEDESTAL FURNITURE DESIGNED BY EERO SAARINEN

79
ハーバート・マター
単脚椅子　1957年頃

Herbert Matter
Single Pedestal Furniture　c. 1957

8
automobiles

An exhibition of motorcar design

The Museum of Modern Art

August 28 to November 11, 1951

76
リオ・リオーニ
8台の自動車デザイン展　1951

Leo Lionni
8 Automobiles　1951

65

81
ハーバート・マター
ジャコメッティ展　1966

Herbert Matter
Giacometti　1966

67

82
エリック・ニッチ
ジェネラル・ダイナミックス　宇宙への第一歩　1955年頃

Erik Nitsche
General Dynamics　First Step into Space　c. 1955

83
エリック・ニッチ
ジェネラル・ダイナミックス　流体力学　1955

Erik Nitsche
General Dynamics　Hydrodynamics　1955

84
エリック・ニッチ
ジェネラル・ダイナミックス　核融合　1958

Erik Nitsche
General Dynamics　Nuclear Fusion　1958

85
エリック・ニッチ
ジェネラル・アトミック　訓練研究原子炉　1958

Erik Nitsch
Triga　General Atomic　1958

86
ルイス・シルバースタイン
WQXR 1955

Louis Silverstein
WQXR 1955

89
ジョージ・クリコリアン
クロスワード・パズルを毎日ニューヨーク・タイムズで　1950

George Krikorian
Crossword Puzzle　Every Day　The New York Times　1950

71

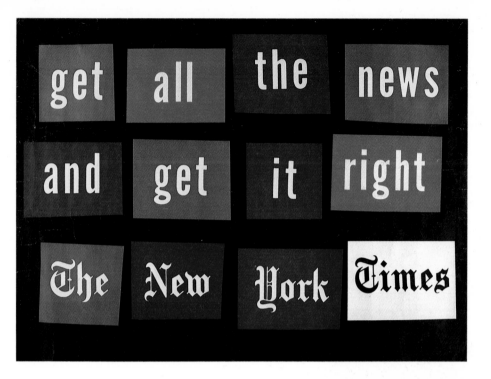

87
ケネス D. ハーク
すべてのニュースを，しかも正確に
ニューヨーク・タイムズ　1951

Kenneth D. Haak
Get All the News and Get It Right
The New York Times　1951

88
ケネス D. ハーク
すべてのニュースを，しかも正確に　ニューヨーク・タイムズ　1951

Kenneth D. Haak
Get All the News and Get It Right　The New York Times　1951

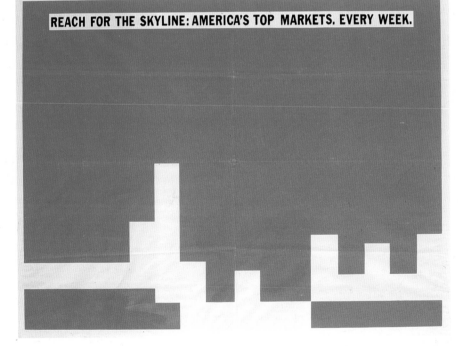

92
デニス・ウィラー
まず〈ライフ〉を開こう　1963年頃

Dennis Wheeler
Any way You Slice It　Life　c. 1963

93
デニス・ウィラー
スカイラインに届く〈ライフ〉　1963

Dennis Wheeler
Reach for the Skyline　Life　1963

90
ソール・バス
映画〈黄金の腕〉　1955

Saul Bass
The Man with the Golden Arm　1955

91
ソール・バス
映画〈ある殺人〉　1959

Saul Bass
Anatomy of a Murder　1959

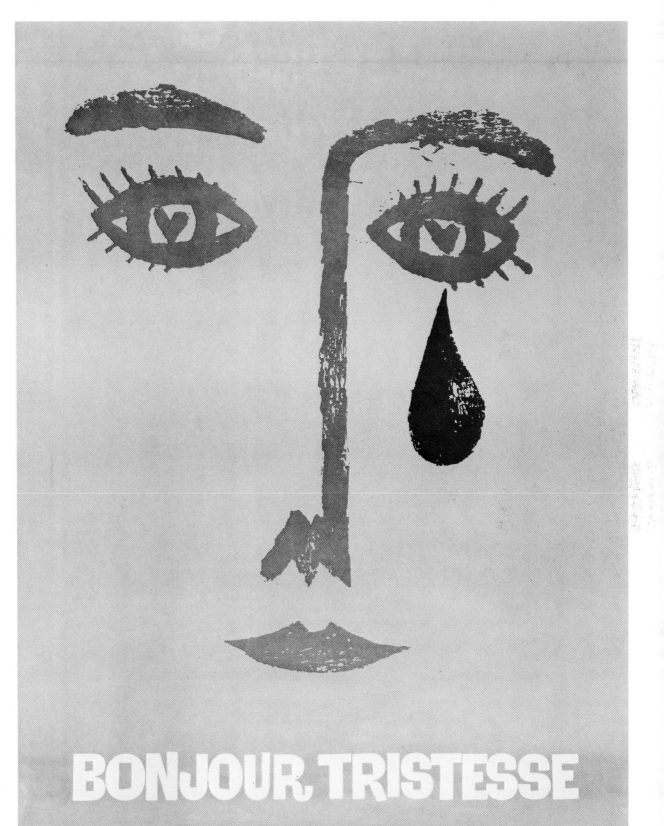

94
ソール・バス
映画〈悲しみよ今日は〉　1957

Saul Bass
Bonjour Tristesse　1957

August 30 thru December 11

95
ロバート・ブランドワイン
ヘンリー・マーコウィッツ
ビッグA（競馬）　8月30日—12月11日　1965

Rebert Brandwein
Henry Markowitz
A　August 30—December 11　1965

96
ルイス・ダンズィガー
メトロポリタン美術館所蔵アメリカ絵画展
1966

Louis Danziger
American Paintings from The Metropolitan
Museum of Art   1966

77

97
ジョージ・チャーニー
スクール・オブ・ヴィジュアル・アート　1959

George Tscherny
School of Visual Arts　1959

98
ジョージ・チャーニー
すべての壁は扉である　1961

George Tscherny
Every Wall Is a Door　1961

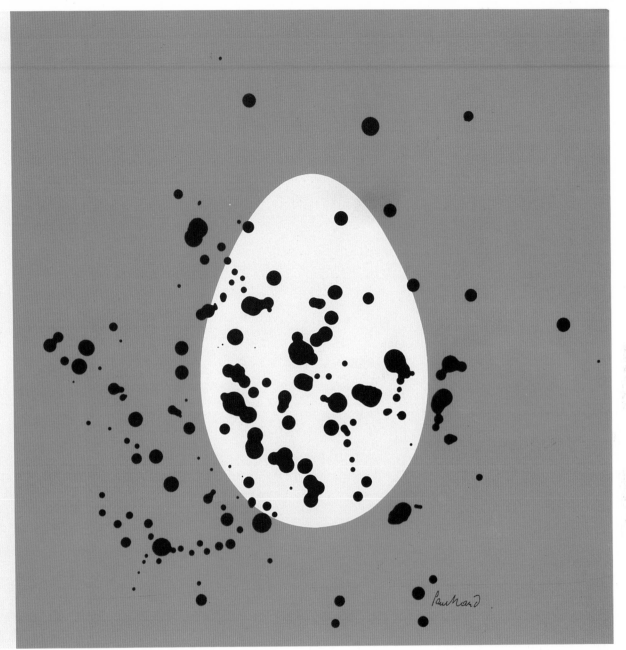

Sources and Resources
of 20th Century Design

June 19 to 24, 1966
The International Design
Conference in Aspen

99
ポール・ランド
20世紀デザインの源泉と現状　1966

Paul Rand
Sources and Resources of 20th Century Design　1966

an Eye for perception, insight, vision.
a Bee for industriousness, dedication, perseverance.
an "M" for motivation, merit, moral strength.

A somewhat unusual perspective of the familiar
IBM logotype, and a light reminder of some of the funda-
mental qualities that have come to characterize
the outstanding men and women who have built, and who
continue to build, the success of the IBM company.

100
ポール・ランド
IBM 1982

Paul Rand
IBM 1982

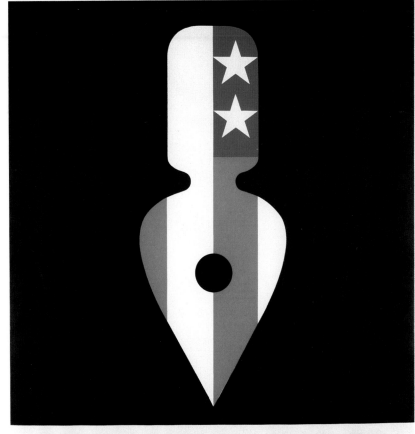

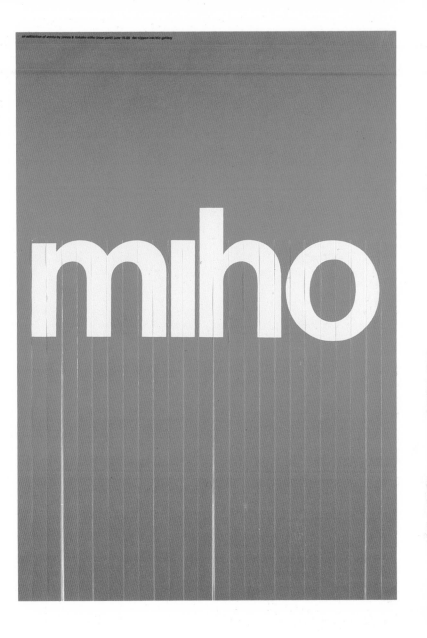

101
アイヴァン・チャーマイエフ
トーマス・ガイズマー
アメリカのグラフィック　1964

Ivan Chermayeff
Thomas Geismar
American Graphics　1964

102
ジェームズ・ミホ
ミホ（個展ポスター）　1972

James Miho
Miho　1972

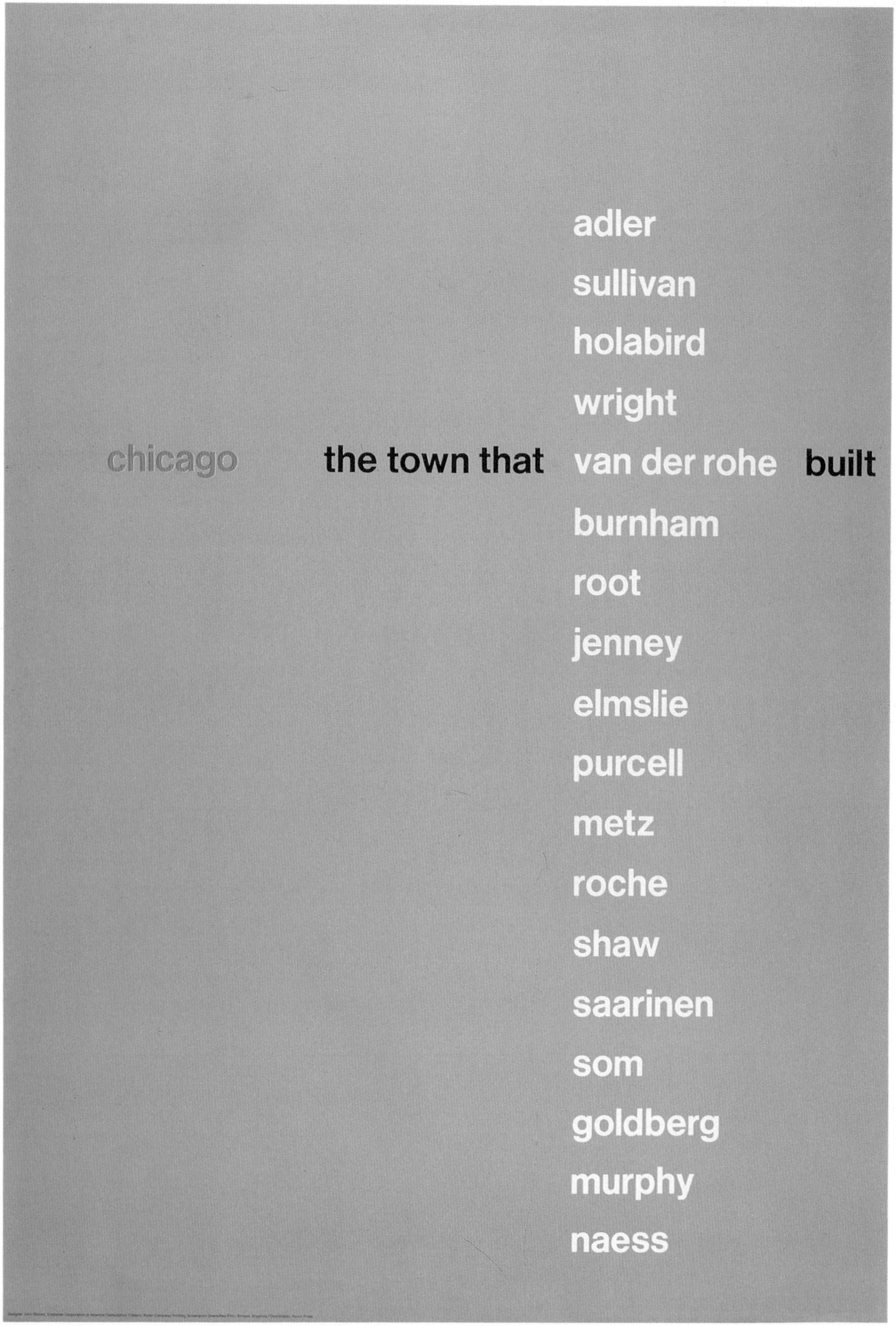

chicago the town that adler sullivan holabird wright van der rohe built burnham root jenney elmslie purcell metz roche shaw saarinen som goldberg murphy naess

103
ジョン・リーベン
シカゴ　ファン・デル・ローエたちの建てた街　1966
John Rieben
Chicago　The Town that Van der Rohe Built　1966

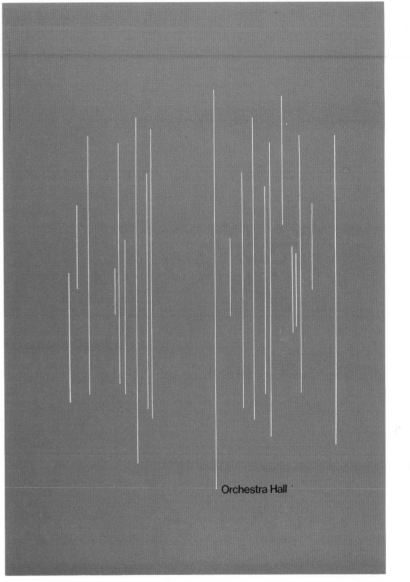

104
ジョン・リーベン
ディアボーン天文台　1966

John Rieben
Dearborn　Observatory　1966

105
ウエストマコット
オーケストラ・ホール　1966

Westmacott
Orchestra Hall　1966

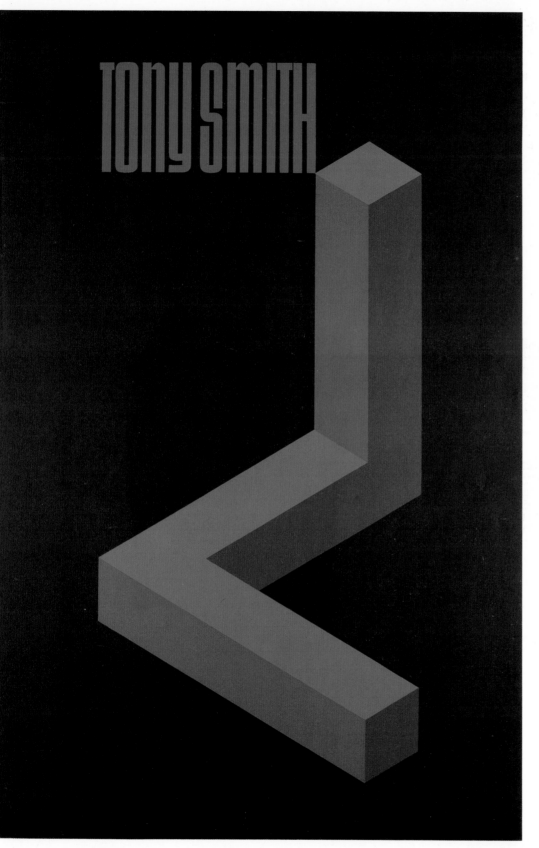

106
ノーマン・アイヴス
トニー・スミス　1967

Norman Ives
Tony Smith　1967

107
ロバート・インディアナ
ロバート・インディアナ展（ステーブル画廊）　1962年10月16日　1962

Robert Indiana
Indiana　Stable　16 October 62　1962

108
ピーター・ジー
ピーター・ジーのグラフィック・デザイン　1966

Peter Gee
Graphic Design　1966

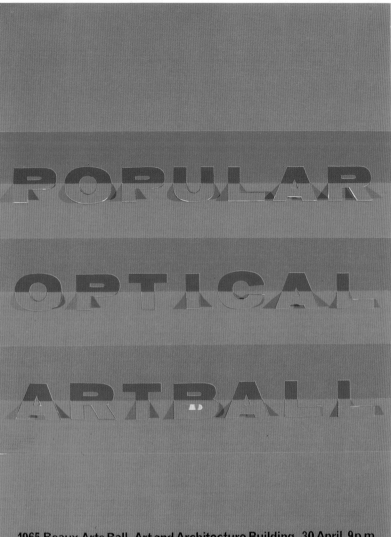

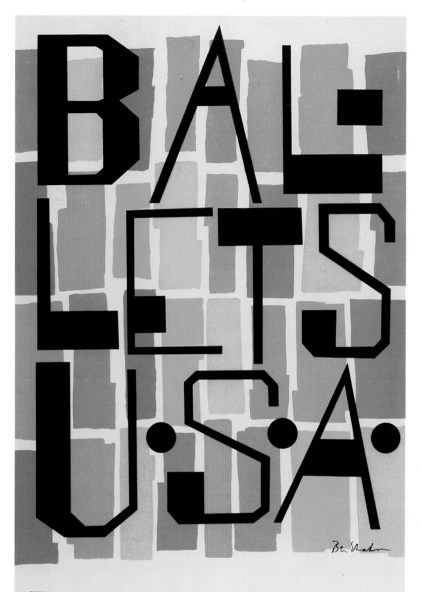

109
ジョン・ナンマン
ポピュラー視覚芸術祭　1965

John Noneman
Popular Optical Artball　1965

111
ベン・シャーン
バレエ　U. S. A.　1959

Ben Shahn
Ballets U. S. A.　1959

110
ハーバート・バイヤー
オリベッティ 1953

Herbert Bayer
Olivetti 1953

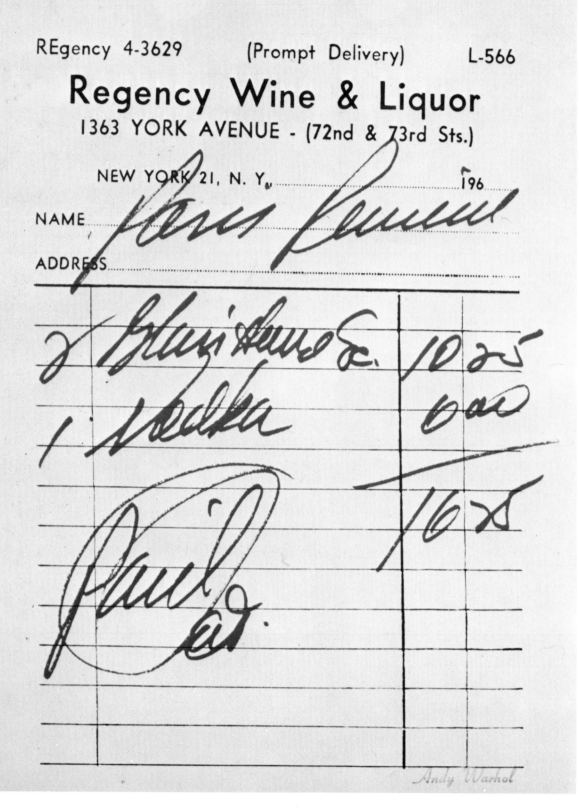

116
アンディ・ウォーホール
パリ・レヴュー 1968

Andy Warhol
Paris Review 1968

115
ピーター・ジー
ピーター・ジー殿　ウエスト・ブロードウェイ506　1963

Peter Gee
Mr. Peter Gee　506 West Broadway　1963

89

114
ピーター・ジー
ピーター・ジー殿　転居　1963

Peter Gee
Peter Gee, Esq.　Not Here　1963

112
アイヴァン・チャーマイエフ
トーマス・ガイズマー
ロバート・ブラウンジョン
リターン・エクシビション（3人によるグラフィッデザインの対話）　1959

Ivan Chermayeff
Thomas Geismar
Robert Brownjohn
A Return Exhibition　1959

113
アイヴァン・チャーマイエフ
目に見えぬ都市　1972

Ivan Chermayeff
The Invisible City　1972

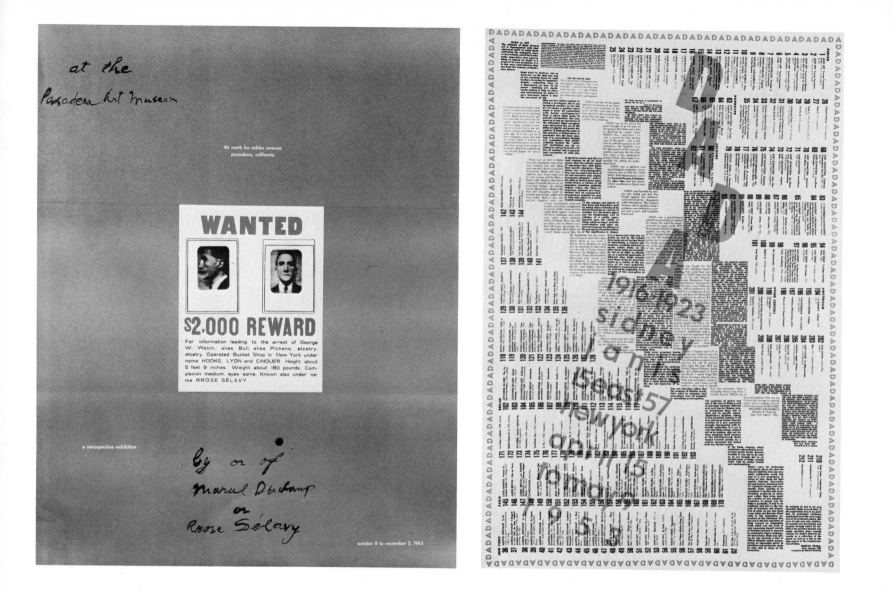

117
マルセル・デュシャン
手配中　賞金2,000ドル（パサデナ美術館におけるマルセル・デュシャン展）　1963

Marcel Duchamp
Wanted　$ 2,000　Reward　1963

118
マルセル・デュシャン
シドニー・ジャニス
ダダ展　1953

Marcel Duchamp
Sidney Janis
DADA　1953

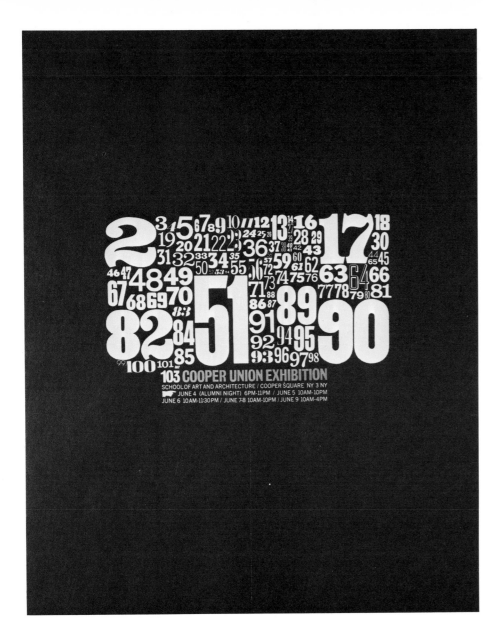

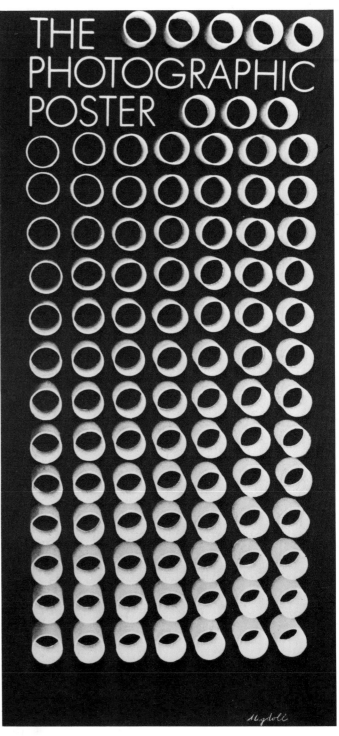

119
ロイ・グレース
103回クーパー・ユニオン展覧会　1962

Roy Grace
103 Cooper Union Exhibition　1962

120
ハーバート・ミグドール
フォトグラフィック・ポスター　1964

Herbert Migdoll
The Photographic Poster　1964

121
ロバート・グレツコ
チャールズ・ズィンマーマン
わが街　1970（ニューヨーク都市デザインのための提案展）　1964

Robert Gretczko
Charles Zimmerman
Our Town 1970　1964

122
ジョン・ミクヴィッカー
アトミズムとフォルム　1965

John McVicker
Atomism and Form　1965

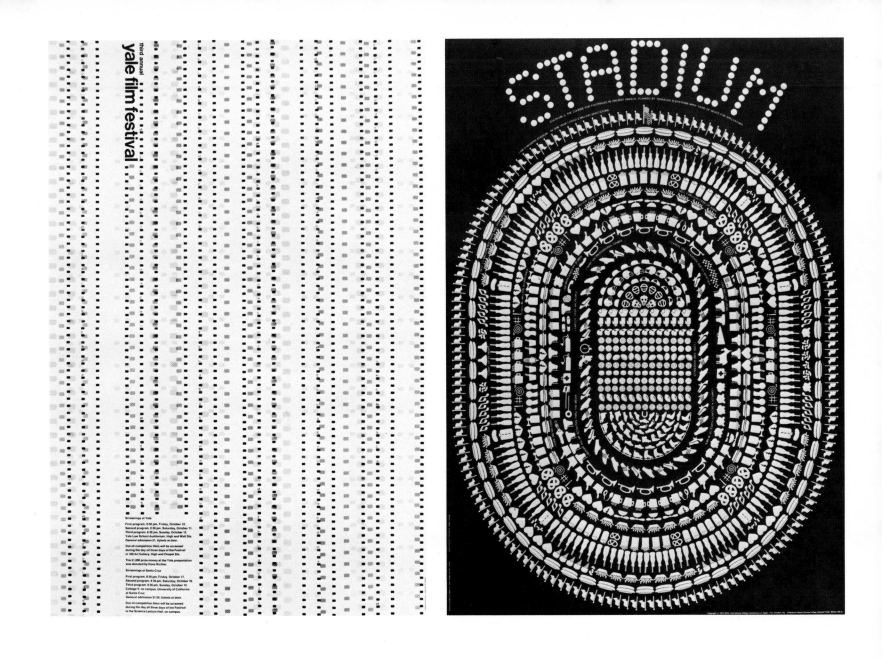

123
ジョエル・カッツ
エール映画祭　1969年頃

Joel Katz
Yale Film Festival　c. 1969

124
ランス・ワイマン
ビル・キャナン
スタジアム　1972

Lance Wyman
Bill Cannan
Stadium　1972

125
モートン・ゴールドショール
アメリカ工業デザイン協会定例会議　1968

Morton Goldsholl
Contradictions　1968

126
H. ランドショフ
不思議の国アメリカへ行こう　1960

H. Landshoff
Visit Wonderland U. S. A.　1960

The First Generation

William Baziotes	Hans Hofmann	Richard Pousette-Dart
Willem De Kooning	Franz Kline	Ad Reinhardt
Arshile Gorky	Robert Motherwell	Mark Rothko
Adolph Gottlieb	Barnett Newman	Clyfford Still
Philip Guston	Jackson Pollock	Bradley Walker Tomlin

Los Angeles County Museum of Art, Lytton Gallery. June 18 through August 1, 1965

Museum Hours: 10-5 Tuesday through Sunday. Closed Monday

Special Hours: The New York School Exhibition will be open Tuesday evenings from 5 until 10 p.m.

Admission Fee: Adults $1.00—Children through 18 years 25¢. Catalogue available

New York School

127
ルイス・ダンズィガー
ニューヨーク・スクールの第一世代展　1965

Louis Danziger
New York School　The First Generation　1965

128
トモコ・ミホ
シカゴの大建築　1967

Tomoko Miho
Great Architecture in Chicago　1967

129
トモコ・ミホ
ニューヨークへの65の橋　1968

Tomoko Miho
65 Bridges to New York　1968

130
ピーター・テューブナー
ハーレム　1968

Peter Teubner
Harlem　1968

131
ピーター・ジー
株式市況　1969年頃

Peter Gee
Market Coverage　c. 1969

132
アンディ・ウォーホール
第5回ニューヨーク映画祭　リンカーン・センター　1967

Andy Warhol
Film Festival　Lincoln Center　1967

133
ピーター・ジー
ブライアント・パーク・フェスティバル　1968

Peter Gee
Bryant Park Festival　1968

134
リー・コンクリン
プロコール・ハラム（コンサート）　1969

Lee Conklin
Procol Harum　1969

135
ヴィクター・モスコソ
ブルー・チアー（ダンス・コンサート）　1967

Victor Moscoso
Blue Cheer　1967

136
ヴィクター・モスコソ
クイックシルバー・メッセンジャー・サーヴィス　1967

Victor Moscoso
Quicksilver Messenger Service　1967

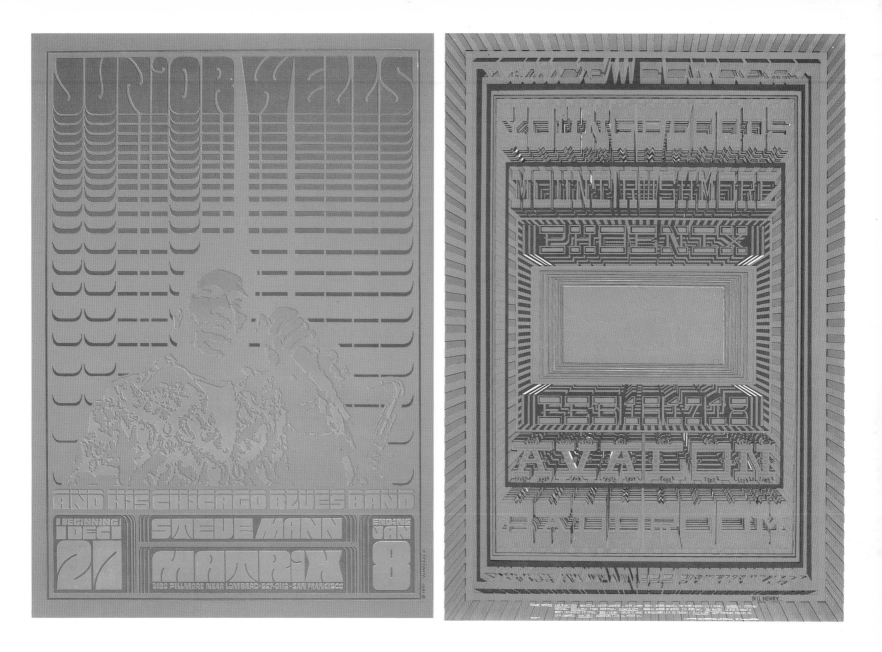

138
ビクター・モスコソ
ジュニア・ウエルズ（コンサート）　1966

Victor Moscoso
Junior Wells　1966

137
ビル・ヘンリー
ヤングブラッヅ（ダンス・コンサート）　1968

Bill Henry
Younglboods　1968

139
ヴィクター・モスコソ
ポール・ユーバック（写真）
オーティス・ラッシュ（コンサート）　1967

Victor Moscoso
Paul Ubac (Photographer)
Otis Rush　1967

140
テッド・シェイン
ターン・オン，チューン・イン，ドロップ・アウト　1967

Ted Shaine
Turn On　Tune In　Drop Out　1967

107

141
スタンリー・マウス
マザーズ・オヴ・インヴェンション（コンサート）　1967

Stanley Mouse
Mothers of Invention　1967

142
ピーター・マックス
キャプテン・ミッドナイト第12号　1966

Peter Max
#12　Captain Midnight　1966

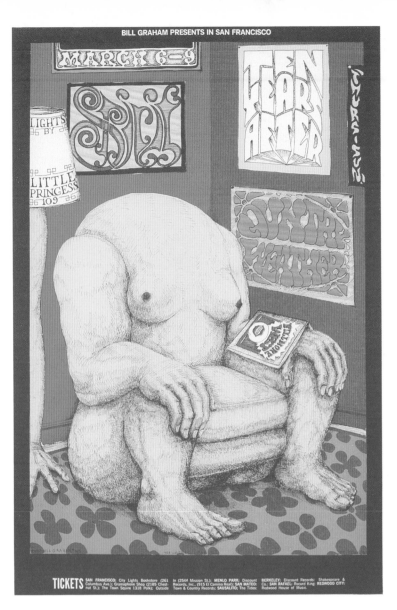

143
リー・コンクリン
テン・イヤーズ・アフター（コンサート）　1969

Lee Conklin
Ten Years After　1969

144
ヴィクター・モスコソ
リーヴァイスで寛ろごう　1967年頃

Victor Moscoso
Rest in Levi's　c. 1967

MADE IN CALIFORNIA

AN EXHIBITION OF FIVE WORKSHOPS
GRUNWALD GRAPHIC ARTS FOUNDATION
U.C.L.A. APRIL 19 - MAY 16, 1971

145
エドワード・ルーシャ
メイド・イン・カリフォルニア　1971

Edward Ruscha
Made in California　1971

147
シーモア・クウァスト
ジュディ・ガーランド（コンサート）　1968

Seymour Chwast
Judy Garland　1968

146
ミルトン・グレイザー
ローヴィン・スプーンフル（コンサート）　1967年頃

Milton Glaser
The Lovin' Spoonful　c. 1967

148
ミルトン・グレイザー
ディラン　1966

Milton Glaser
Dylan　1966

149
C. H. ジョハンスン
ヴィジョンズ　1967

C. H. Johansen
Visions　1967

150
ディヴィッド・ウィルコックス
ニーナ・シモーヌ　1970

David Wilcox
Nina Simone　1970

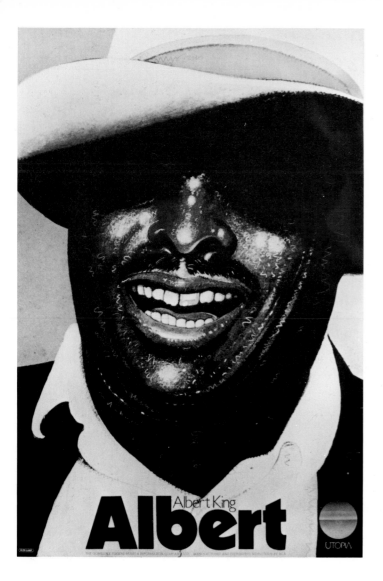

152
ミルトン・グレイザー
アルバート・キング　1976

Milton Glaser
Albert　1976

151
ミルトン・グレイザー
マハリア・ジャクスン（コンサート）　1967

Milton Glaser
Mahalia Jackson　1967

It's the real thing

Napalm

16 FL. OZ.

TRADE-MARK ®
UNITED STATES

for S.E. Asia

153
クリストス・ジャナコス
青年たちを国へ還そう　1966

Christos Gianakos
Send Our Boys Home　1966

115

155
作者不明
こいつは東南アジア向けの本物だ　1970年頃

Unknown
It's the Real Thing for S. E. Asia　c. 1970

156
ピーター・ブラント
R. L. ハーバリィ（写真）
問：そして，赤ん坊も？
答：そして，赤ん坊も。　1970

Peter Brandt
R. L. Haeberle (Photographer)
Q.　And Babies?　A.　And Babies.　1970

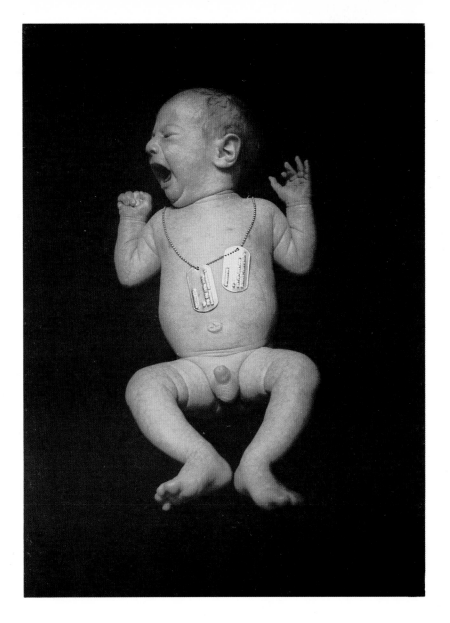

154
シーモア・クウァスト
臭い息を止めよ 1967

Seymour Chwast
End Bad Breath 1967

157
ハワード・ブルーム
ロン・ポロウスキー
ロバート・モンドロック（写真）
無　題 1968

Howard Blume
Ron Borowski
Robert Mondlock (Photographer)
Untitled 1968

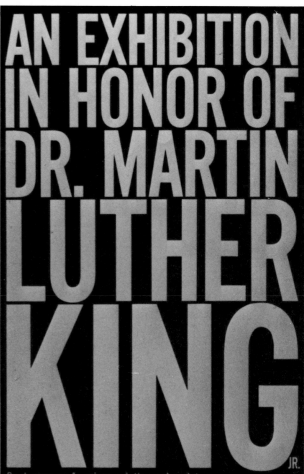

158
ピーター・ジー
自由，平等　1968

Peter Gee
Freedom　Equality　1968

159
ピーター・ジー
マーチン・ルサー・キング博士　1968

Peter Gee
Dr. Martin Luther King　1968

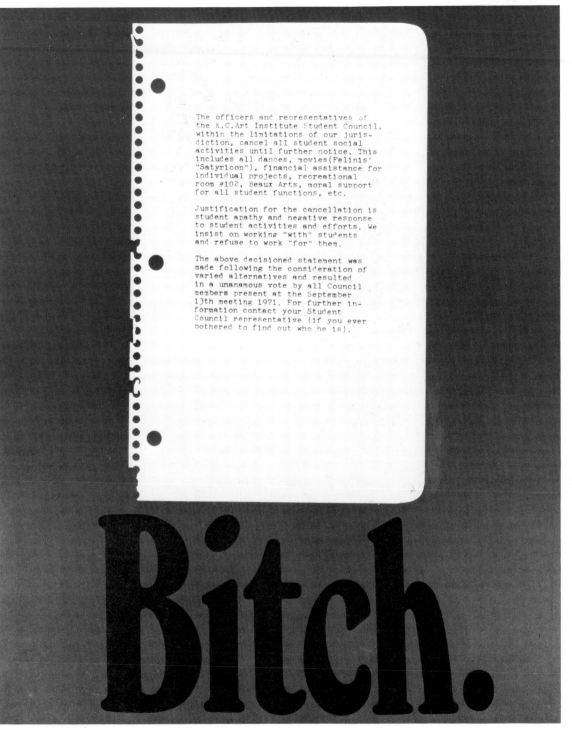

160
コンラッド
畜生め　1971

Conrad
Bitch　1971

161
ロバート・マイルズ・ランヤン
第17回アスペン国際デザイン会議　1967

Robert Miles Runyan
17th International Design Conference in Aspen　1967

162
ラリー・リバーズ
第1回ニューヨーク映画祭　1963

Larry Rivers
First New York Film Festival　1963

163
ジム・ダイン
シティー・センター　ギルバート・アンド・サリバン　1968

Jim Dine
City Center　Gilbert & Sullivan　1968

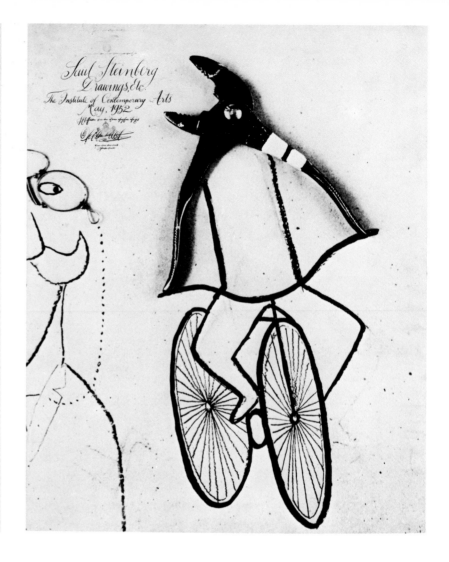

164
アレクサンダー・コールダー
コールダー・サーカス　1972

Alexander Calder
Calder's Circus　1972

165
ソール・スタインバーグ
ドローイング，その他（個展ポスター）　1952

Saul Steinberg
Drawings, Etc.　1952

166
ソール・スタインバーグ
マーグ・ファンデーションの夕べ　1970

Saul Steinberg
Nuits de la Foundation Maeght　1970

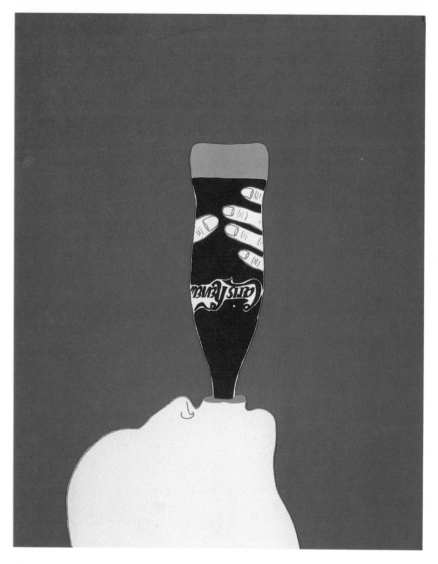

167
ソール・スタインバーグ
スポレト・フェスティバル　1969

Saul Steinberg
Spoleto Festival　1969

168
マリソール・エスコバール
パリ・レビュー　1967

Marisol Escobar
Paris Review　1967

169
ジャスパー・ジョーンズ
ジャスパー・ジョーンズ展　2月24日—3月16日
於：レオ・カステリ画廊　1968

Jasper Johns
J. Johns　24 Feb.—16 March　Leo Castelli　1968

125

171
フランク・ステラ
リンカーン・センター・フェスティバル'67　1967

Frank Stella
Lincoln Center Festival '67　1967

170
ロイ・リクテンスタイン
リンカーン・センター（第4回ニューヨーク・フィルム・
フェスティバル） 1966

Roy Lichtenstein
Lincoln Center 1966

172
リチャード・リンドナー
アルトゥーロ・ウイの三日天下　1968

Richard Lindner
The Resistable Rise of Arturo Ui　1968

173
ポール・デーヴィス
三文オペラ　1976

Paul Davis
Three Penny Opera　1976

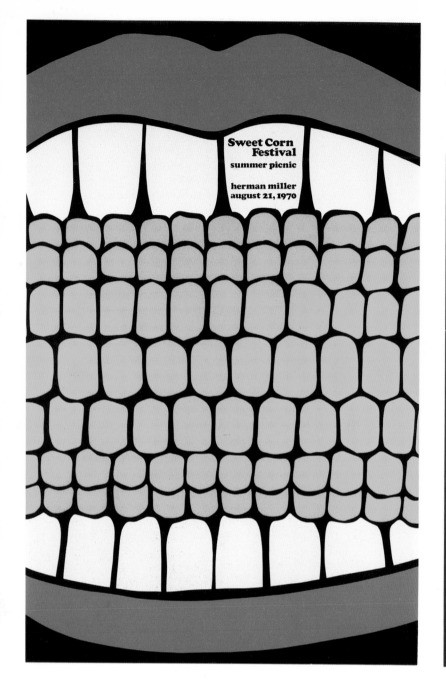

174
スティーヴン・フライコルム
スイート・コーン・フェスティバル　1970

Stephen Frykholm
Sweet Corn Festival　1970

175
スティーヴン・フライコルム
ハーマン・ミラー　サマー・ピクニック'74　1974

Stephen Frykholm
Herman Miller　Summer　Picnic '74　1974

176
スティーヴン・フライコルム
ハーマン・ミラー　サマー・ピクニック'75　1975

Stephen Frykholm
Herman Miller　Summer Picnic '75　1975

177
スティーヴン・フライコルム
ハーマン・ミラー　サマー・ピクニック'77　1977

Stephen Frykholm
Herman Miller　Summer Picnic '77　1977

178
スティーヴン・フライコルム
ハーマン・ミラー　サマー・ピクニック'78　1978

Stephen Frykholm
Herman Miller　Summer Picnic '78　1978

179
スティーヴン・フライコルム
ハーマン・ミラー　サマー・ピクニック'80　1980

Stephen Frykholm
Herman Miller　Summer Picnic '80　1980

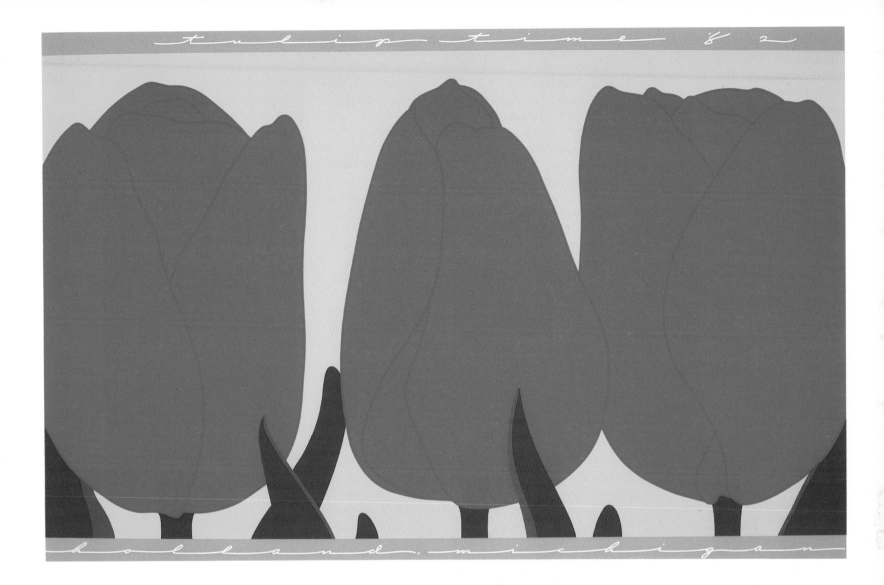

180
スティーヴン・フライコルム
ミシガン州ホーランドのチューリップ　1982

Stephen Frykholm
Tulip Time '82　Holland, Michigan　1982

181
アイヴァン・チャーマイエフ
トーマス・ガイズマー
パン・ナムでバリ島へ　1972

Ivan Chermayeff
Thomas Geismar
Pan Am　Bali　1972

182
アイヴァン・チャーマイエフ
トーマス・ガイズマー
パン・ナムで日本へ　1972

Ivan Chermayeff
Thomas Geismar
Pan Am　Japan　1972

Visit the NY Aquarium

MTA gets you there

Subway:
West 8th Street
Ⓕ
Ⓜ Mon-Fri
Ⓓ Sat Sun Holidays

Bus:
B36 B49
B68

Transit Telephone
212 852 5000

Save time, Save money
Save energy

Ⓜ Metropolitan
Transportation
Authority

183
マイケル・ボスニヤック
ハワード・ヨーク
ラス・キニイ（写真）
ニューヨーク水族館へ行こう　1974

Michael Bosniak
Howard York
Russ Kinne (Photographer)
Visit the NY Aquarium　1974

184
パトリック・カニンガム
ティモシー・ハースリー（写真）
近代建築の変遷　1979

Patrick Cunningham
Timothy Hursley (Photographer)
Transformations in Modern Architecture　1979

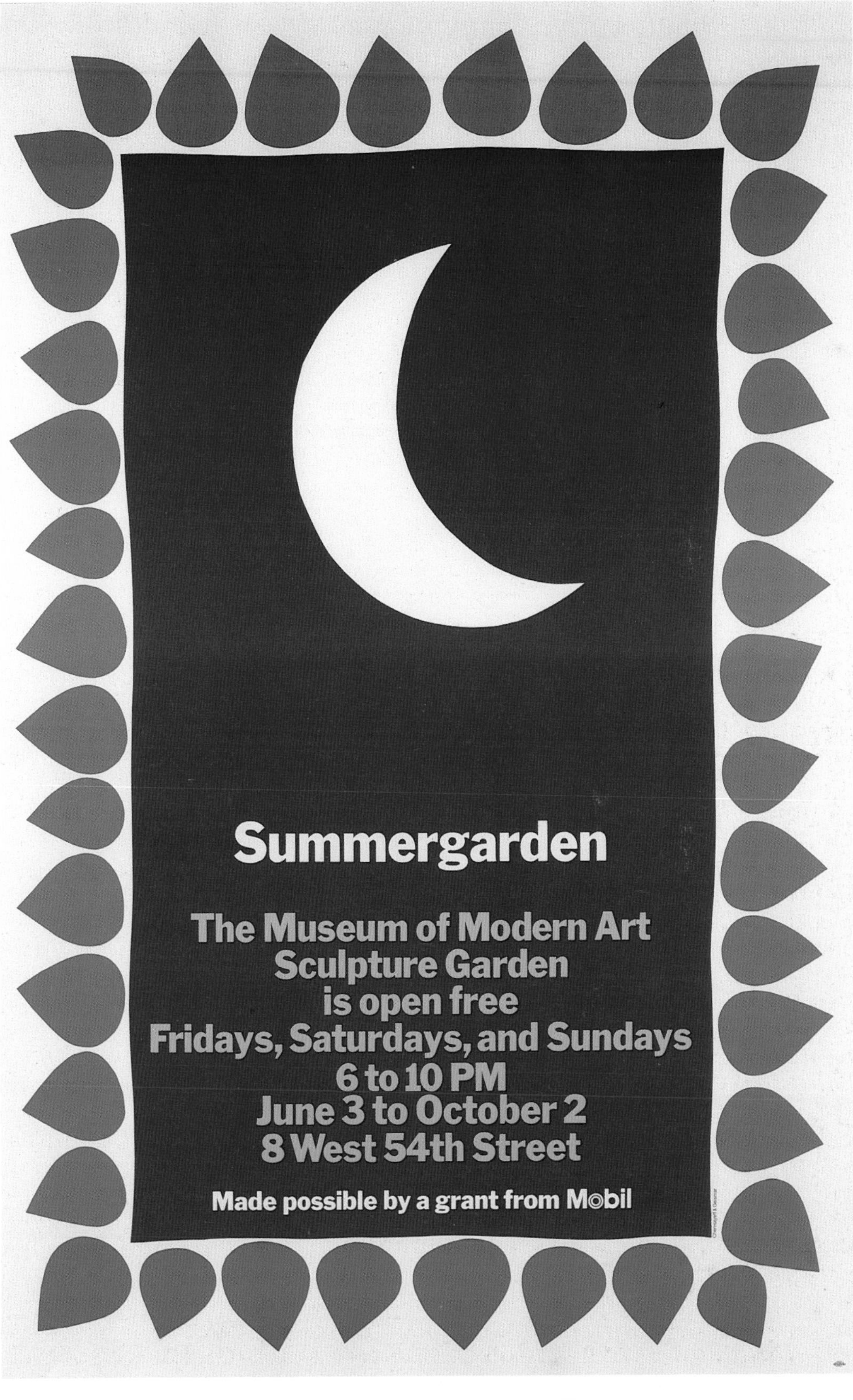

185
アイヴァン・チャーマイエフ
トーマス・ガイズマー
サマー・ガーデン　1978

Ivan Chermayeff
Thomas Geismar
Summergarden　1978

187
ミルトン・グレーザー
ビッグ・ヌード　1968

Milton Glaser
Big Nudes　1968

186
ミルトン・グレーザー
シーモア・クウァスト
アンブレイカブル（プッシュピン・スタジオの15年展）　1971

Milton Glaser
Seymour Chwast
Unbreakable　1971

188
フィリップ・ギップス
エマニュエル夫人（映画） 1974

Phillip Gips
Emanuelle 1974

189

フランセス・バトラー

日本のグラフィック・デザイン―現代　1972

Frances Butler

Japanese Graphic Design, Contemporary　1972

Want a poster? Write 7UP Poster Offer,
P.O. Box 16061, St. Louis Missouri, 63105

193
ロバート・エイブル
セブン・アップ 1975

Robert Abel
7Up 1975

192
シーモア・クウァスト
わが芸術に歌えば　1976

Seymour Chwast
With a Song in My Art　1976

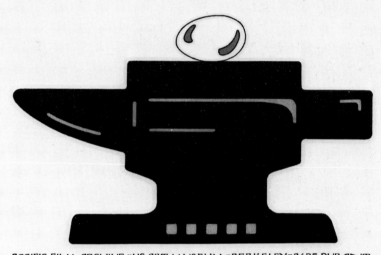

190
デイヴィッド・ランス・ゴーインズ
嘆きの天使　1973

David Lance Goines
Der Blaue Engel　1973

191
ギルバート・レサー
エクワス（劇場ドラマ）　1974

Gilbert Lesser
Equus　1974

141

194

チャールズ・ホワイト三世
ご来場の皆さん　ローリング・ストーンズです　1974

Charles White III
Ladies and Gentlemen　The Rolling Stones　1974

195
キット・ヒンリックス
カリフォルニア・アメリカ・グラフィック・アーティスト協会　1982

Kit Hinrichs
AIGA　California Design　1982

143

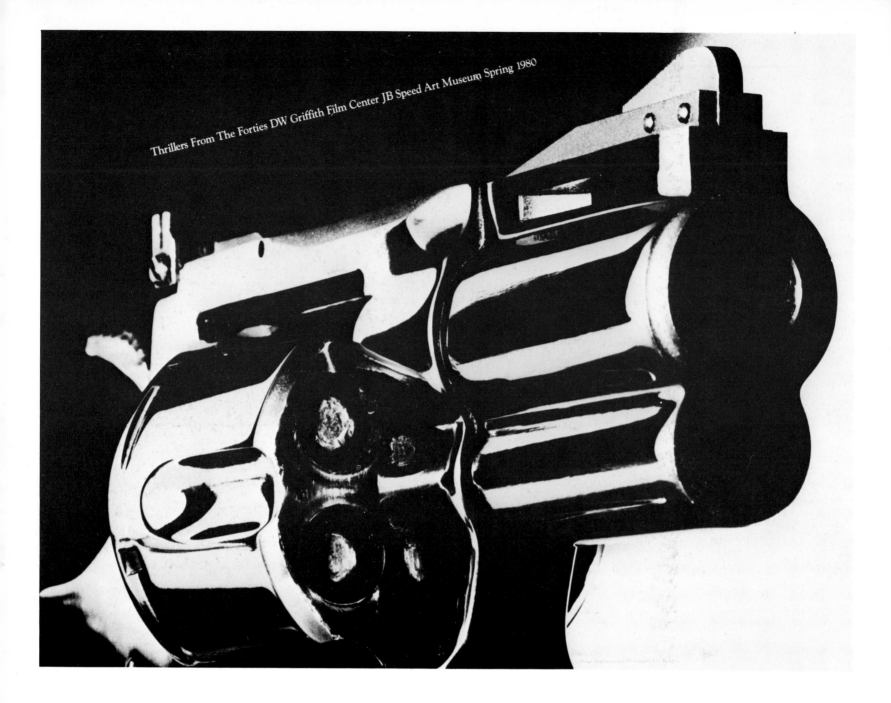

Thrillers From The Forties DW Griffith Film Center JB Speed Art Museum Spring 1980

196
ジューリアス・フリードマン
1940年代のスリラー　1980

Julius Friedman
Thrillers from the Forties　1980

PHOTOGRAPHY MANARCHY
LITHOGRAPHY HENNEGAN

197
ジェフ・バーンズ
デニス・マナーキー（写真）
写真　マナーキー　リトグラフィー　ヘネガン　1980

Jeff Barnes
Dennis Manarcy (Photographer)
Photography Manarcy　Lithography Hennegan　1980

198
ジョン・ミクヴィッカー
ボブ・パイク（写真）
ビッグＡ（競馬）　10月28日—12月10日　1970

John McVicker
Bob Pike (Photographer)
Big A　Oct. 28—Dec. 10　1970

THE THRILL IS BACK.
Aqueduct Opens Feb. 24. First race 1:30.

199
ジョン・ミクヴィッカー
あの興奮が戻って来る　1970年頃

John McVicker
The Thrill is Back　c. 1970

147

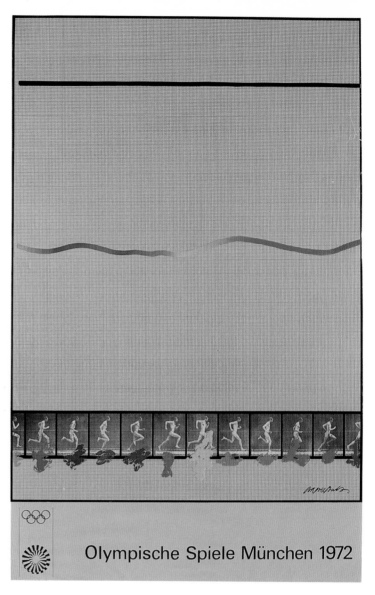

200
フィリップ・ギップス
スウェーデン製品　1973

Philip Gips
Imported from Sweden　1973

201
荒川修作
ミュンヘン・オリンピック　1972

Shusaku Arakawa
Olympische Spiele München　1972

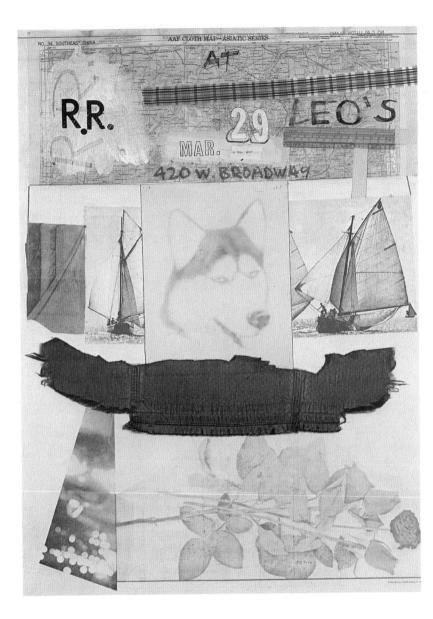

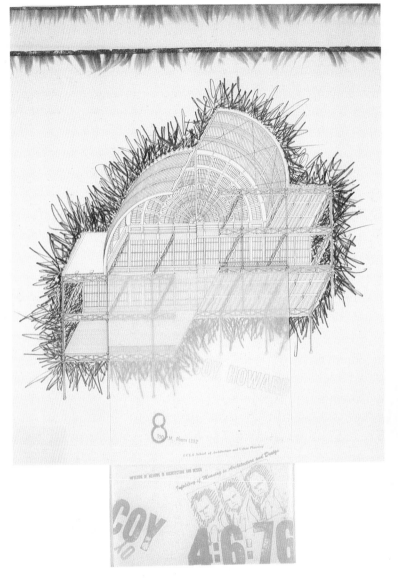

202
ロバート・ラウシェンバーグ
レオ・キャスティリ画廊でのロバート・ラウシェンバーグ展　1980

Robert Rauschenberg
R. R. at Leo's　1980

203
コイ・ハワード
コイ・ハワード〈建築とデザインに内包される多重な意味〉　1976

Coy Howard
Coy Howard　Infolding of Meaning in Architecture and Design　1976

149

204
ジャック・ボイントン
レトロ＝スペクトラム（展覧会ポスター） 1980

Jack Boynton
Retro-Spectrum 1980

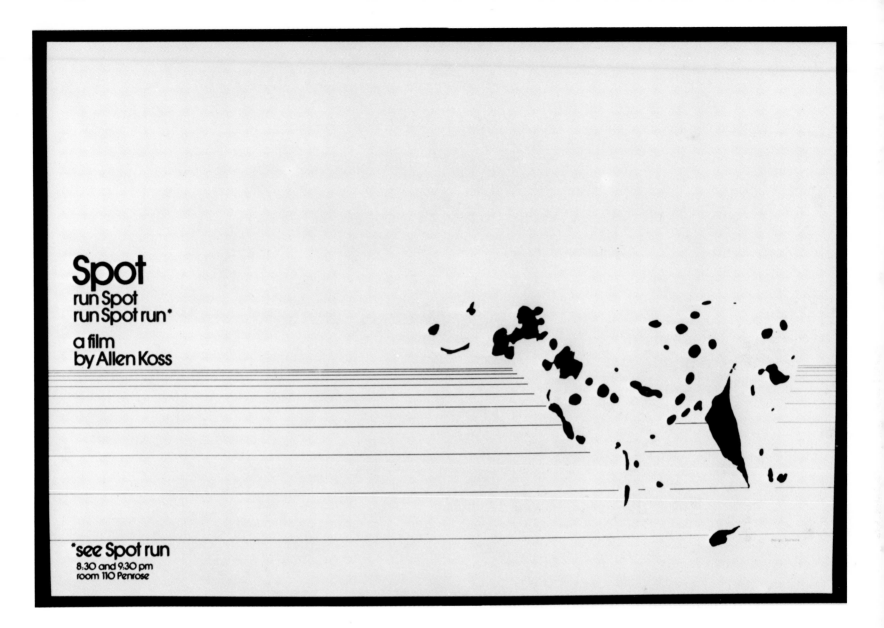

205
ジョー・スコーソニィ
スポット・ラン　スポット・ラン（映画）　1974

Joe Scorsone
Spot Run Spot Run　1974

151

206
アイヴァン・チャーマイエフ
トーマス・ガイズマー
ニューヨーク・フィルハーモニー　1978

Ivan Chermayeff
Thomas Geismar
The New York Philharmonic　1978

207
ジョージ・チャーニー
19世紀のドイツ　1981

George Tscherny
Germany in the 19th Century 1981

BORROMINI PIRANDELLO BARBERINI VIGNELLI
MORAVIA BOCCIONI COLOMBO PUCCINI RADICE
CROCE DE CARLO PERUZZI CIMABUE PALLADIO
AULENTI GALILEO BRAMANTE BALLA ARMANI
RAGGI MENOTTI FELLINI MENDINI PININFARINA
PAGANINI GIORGIONE NOORDA BERNINI VASARI
CARAVAGGIO BURRI PIRANESI PIERO GIUGIARO
MADERNO NERVI NERONE PASOLINI DONIZETTI
ROSSI TOSCANINI LEOPARDI AGNELLI FERRARI
ORSINI VERDI DONATELLO CENCI SAVONAROLA
FIORUCCI ZEFFIRELLI LIPPI GREGOTTI GUCCI
MAZZEI BRION CERATTO VOLTA SPQR ZANUSO
STRADIVARI GIURGOLA VALENTINO PETRARCA
BRUNELLESCHI BOTTICELLI SCOLA BOCCACCIO
MODIGLIANI CARUSO MANGIONE DE BENEDETTI
GRUCCI CASTAGNOLI PIANO LEONARDO CELLINI
SOTTSASS BERTOLUCCI FERMI CHIGI CASANOVA
BORGIA MARINETTI VALLE ANTONIONI MEDICI
MASACCIO ZEVI ALBERTI WOJTYLA CICERONE
CESARE GARIBALDI BELLINI RESPIGHI MAZZINI
SARTOGO VESPUCCI BENE FALLACI BORGHESE
MACHIAVELLI BARZINI CANOVA SOAVI NICOLAO
FARNESE GIOTTO LOLLOBRIGIDA ECO ROSSINI
CASSINA MARCONI TIZIANO MISSONI ARBASINO
TINTORETTO VILLAGIO VIVALDI QUILICI PESCE
BUGATTI LIONNI BILLESI PECCEI MONTESSORI
RAFFAELLO BODONI OLIVETTI MICHELANGELO
DANTE ETCETERA ETCETERA THE ITALIAN IDEA

INTERNATIONAL DESIGN CONFERENCE IN ASPEN 1981   JUNE 14 TO 19

Rufus Porter Rediscovered:
Artist, Inventor, Journalist
1792-1884

The Hudson River Museum   April 12 July 6, 1980
Trevor Park-on-Hudson
Yonkers, New York

208
ジョージ・セデック
イタリアのアイディア　1981

George Sadek
The Italian Idea　1981

209
ルードルフ・デ・ハラク
フランク・ベネディクト
ルーファス・ポーター再発見　1980

Rudolph de Harak
Frank Benedict
Rufus Porter Rediscovered　1980

The World of Otis

East Building
National Gallery of Art
Washington, D.C.

"Art, architecture, craftsmanship all come together to create the true and triumphant expression of our time."

Architect: I. M. Pei Associates
Builder: Charles H. Tompkins Company

Elevators and Escalators by Otis

210
アーノルド・サクス
インゴ・シャーレンブロイク
ジェイ・メーゼル（写真）
オーティスの世界　1981

Arnold Saks
Ingo Scharrenbroich
Jay Maisel (Photographer)
The World of Otis　1981

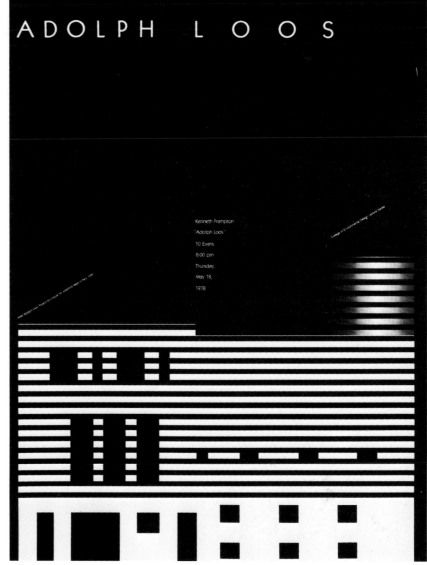

211
ジョン・カサド
ジャン・マルク　1980

John Casado
Jeanne Marc　1980

212
マルク・トゥライヴ
アードルフ・ロス　1978

Marc Treib
Adolph Loos　1978

155

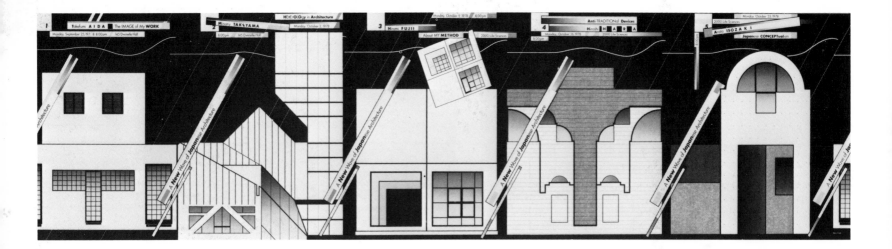

213

マルク・トゥライブ
日本建築の新しい波　1978

Marc Treib
New Wave of Japanese Architecture　1978

出品目録
Catalog

ロバート・エイブル

193

セブン・アップ　1975
オフセット・リトグラフ
115×151 cm

ミルトン・エィコフ　b.1915

67

差別を無くそう　1949
オフセット・リトグラフ
111.5×83.2 cm

71

小児麻痺の治療を皆んなに　1949
オフセット・リトグラフ
116×73.7 cm

ヴィクター・アンコナ

55　カール・カーラーの項参照

荒川修作　b. 1936

201

ミュンヘン・オリンピック　1972
オフセット・リトグラフ
101×64 cm

ジョン・アサートン　b.1900

59

不用意なひと言が墓標をふやす　1943
オフセット・リトグラフ
101×72 cm

ウィリアム・オールバック＝リヴィ
1889—1964

Robert Abel

193

7UP　1975
Offset Lithograph　45 1/2 × 59 1/2 in
Gift of Leslie Schreyer

Milton Ackoff　b.1915

67

Wipe out Discrimination　1949
Offset Llthograph　43 7/8 × 32 3/4 in
Gift of the Congress of lndustrial
Organizations

71

Polio Care Open to All　1949
Offset Lithograph　45 5/8 × 29 in
Gift of the lnfantile Paralysis Founda-
tion

Victor Ancona

See Koehler, Ancona

Shusaku Arakawa　b.1936

201

Olympische Spiele München　1972
Offset Lithograph　39 3/4 × 25 1/4 in
Gift of Edition Olympia

John Atherton　b.1900

59

A Careless Word　　Another Cross
1943
Offset Lithograph　39 3/4 × 28 3/8 in
Gift of the Office of War lnformation

William Auerbach-Levy
1889-1964

34

アル・ジョルスン〈ジャズ・シンガー〉
1927
シルクスクリーン
71×56 cm

ジェフ・バーンズ　b.1947
デニス・マナーキー（写真）
b.1943

197

写真　マナーキー
リトグラフィー　ヘネガン　1980
オフセット・リトグラフ
49.5×77.5 cm

ソール・バス　b.1921

90

映画〈黄金の腕〉　1955
オフセット・リトグラフ
103×68.7 cm

91

映画〈ある殺人〉　1959
オフセット・リトグラフ
104×68 cm

94

映画〈悲しみよ今日は〉　1957
オフセット・リトグラフ
82.5×63 cm

ハーバート・バイヤー　b.1900

70

小児麻痺研究　1949
オフセット・リトグラフ
113×73 cm

34

Al Jolson　"The Jazz Singer"　1927
Silkscreen　28 × 22 in
Mark del Costello Collection
Gift of Celeste Bartos

Jeff Barnes　b.1947
Dennis Manarchy (Photographer)
b.1943

197

Photography Manarchy　　Lithography
Hennegan　1980
Offset Lithograph　19 1/2 × 30 1/2 in
Gift of the designer

Saul Bass　b.1921

90

The Man with the Golden Arm　1955
Offset Lithograph　40 1/2 × 27 in
Gift of Otto Preminger Productions,
United Artists

91

Anatomy of a Murder　1959
Offset Lithograph　41 × 26 3/4 in
Gift of Otto Preminger Productions,
United Artists

94

Bonjour Tristesse　1957
Offset Lithograph　32 1/2 × 24 3/4 in
Gift of the designer

Herbert Bayer　b.1900

70

Polio Research　1949
Offset Lithograph　44 1/2 × 28 3/4 in
Gift of the lnfantile Paralysis Founda-
tion

110
オリベッティ　1953
オフセット・リトグラフ
70×50 cm

110
Olivetti　1953
Offset Lithograph　27 1/2 × 19 5/8 in
Gift of the designer

レスター・ビヨー　1903—1969

38
水道を（農務省農村電化促進局）　1937
シルクスクリーン
101.6×76.2 cm

39
ラジオを（農務省農村電化促進局）　1937
シルクスクリーン
102×76.2 cm

40
農作業の機械化を（農務省農村電化促進局）　1937
シルクスクリーン
101.5×76.5 cm

41
電灯を（農務省農村電化促進局）　1937
シルクスクリーン
101.8×76.2 cm

66
スラム街が犯罪の温床となる　1941
オフセット・リトグラフ
100.5×75 cm

フランク・ベネディクト
209　ルドールフ・デ・ハラクの項参照

ジョーゼフ・ビンダー　1898—1972

42
一番大切な車輪　1951
オフセット・リトグラフ
71.3×56 cm

Lester Beall　1903-1969

38
Running Water　1937
Silkscreen　40 × 30 in
Gift of the designer

39
Radio　1937
Silkscreen　40 1/4 × 30 in
Gift of the designer

40
Farm Work　1937
Silkscreen　40 × 30 1/8 in
Gift of the designer

41
Light　1937
Silkscreen　40 × 30 in
Gift of the designer

66
Slums Breed Crime　1941
Offset Lithograph　39 5/8 × 29 1/2 in
Gift of the designer

Frank Benedict
See de Harak, Benedict

Joseph Binder　1898-1972

42
The Most Important Wheels　1951
Offset Lithograph　28 1/8 × 22 in
Gift of the designer

43
合衆国陸軍航空隊　1941
テンペラ
101.7×76.2 cm

ハワード・ブルーム
ロン・ボロウスキー
ロバート・モンドロック（写真）

157
無　題
オフセット・リトグラフ
69.8×50.8 cm

ロン・ボロウスキー
157　ハワード・ブルームの項参照

マイケル・ボスニヤック　b.1947
ハワード・ヨーク　b.1943
ラス・キニィ（写真）　b.1928

183
ニューヨーク水族館へ行こう　1974
オフセット・リトグラフ
106.7×151.2 cm

ジャック・ボイントン　b.1928

204
レトロ＝スペクトラム（展覧会ポスター）
1980
オフセット・リトグラフ
75×56 cm

ウィル・ブラッドレー　1868—1962

2
チャップブック　1895
リトグラフ
53.8×35 cm

43
Air Corps U. S. Army　1941
Tempera　40 × 30 in
Gift of the designer

Howard Blume
Ron Borowski
Robert Mondlock (Photographer)

157
Unitled　1968
Offset Lithograph　27 1/2 × 20 in
Gift of the designers

Ron Borowski
See Blume, Borowski, Mondlock

Michael Bonsiak　b.1947
Howard York　b.1943
Russ Kinne (Photographer)
b.1928

183
Visit the NY Aquarium　1974
Offset Lithograph　42 × 59 1/2 in
Poster Fund

Jack Boynton　b.1928

204
Retro-Spectrum　1980
Offset Lithograph　29 1/2 × 22 in
Gift of the Amarillo Art Center

Will Bradley　1868-1962

2
The Chap Book　1895
Lithograph　21 1/4 × 13 3/4 in
Exchange

3
ホワイティングの標準紙　　1900年頃
リトグラフ
50.5×23.2 cm

4
チャップブック　5月号　　1895
リトグラフ
55.7×40.7 cm

5
チャップブック　　1895
リトグラフ
47.7×33 cm

6
チャップブック　感謝祭号　　1895
リトグラフ
52.5×35.6 cm

7
ウィル・ブラッドレーの本　　1896
木版
106.8×73.3 cm

ピーター・ブラント
R. L. ハーバリィ（写真）

156
問：そして，赤ん坊も？
答：そして，赤ん坊も。　　1970
オフセット・リトグラフ
63.8×96.5 cm

ロバート・ブランドワイン
1933—1972
ヘンリー・マーコウィッツ　b.1930

95
ビッグA（競馬）　8月30日―12月11日
1965
オフセット・リトグラフ
114×150 cm

3
Whiting's Standard Papers　　c. 1900
Lithograph　19 7/8 × 9 1/16 in
Exchange

4
The Chap Book　　May　　1895
Lithograph　21 15/16 × 16 in
Exchange

5
The Chap Book　　1895
Lithograph　18 3/4 × 13 in
Exchange

6
The Chap Book　　Thanksgiving No.
1895
Lithograph　20 3/4 × 14 in
Exchange

7
Bradley　　His Book　　1896
Woodcut　42 × 28 7/8 in
Exchange

Peter Brandt
R. L. Haeberle (Photographer)

156
Q. And Babies?　　A.　And　Babies.
1970
Offset Lithograph　25 1/8 × 38 in
Gift of the Benefit for the Attica
Defense Fund

Robert Brandwein　　1933–1972
Henry Markowitz　b.1930

95
A　　August 30-December 11　　1965
Offset Lithograph　44 7/8 × 59 1/16 in
Gift of the New York Racing Association

L. N. ブリットン

27
もっと食べよ　節食せよ　　1917年頃
リトグラフ
72.3×51.7 cm

ハーブ・ブラウン

75
ハーブ・ブラウン個展ポスター　　1965
オフセット，シルクスクリーン併用
108.7×75.5 cm

ロバート・ブラウンジョン
112　アイヴァン・チャーマイエフの項参照

ブルベーカー

33
グッド・ブック　　1927年頃
リトグラフ
53.5×34.3 cm

フランセス・バトラー

189
日本のグラフィック・デザイン―現代
1972
シルクスクリーン，ステッカー貼付
59.5×47 cm

アレクサンダー・コールダー
1898—1976

164
コールダー・サーカス　　1972
オフセット・リトグラフ
91.5×69.7 cm

L. N. Britton

27
Eat More　　Eat Less　　c. 1917
Lithograph　28 1/2 × 20 3/8 in
Exchange

Herb Brown

75
Herb Brown　　1965
Silkscreen over offset lithograph
42 3/4 × 29 3/4 in
Gift of the designer

Robert Brownjohn
See Chermayeff, Geismar, Brownjohn

Brubaker

33
A Good Book　　c. 1927
Lithograph　21 × 13 1/2 in
Exchange

Frances Butler

189
Japanese Graphic Design, Contemporary
1972
Silkscreen with decorative stickers
23 1/2 × 18 1/2 in
Gift of the designer

Alexander Calder　1898-1976

164
Calder's Circus　　1972
Offset Lithograph　36 × 27 1/2 in
Gift of Peter Stone

ビル・キャナン
124 ランス・ワイマンの項参照

Bill Cannan
See Wyman, Cannan

ジョン・カルル b.1900

45
アメリカの回答！ 生産 1942
オフセット・リトグラフ
76×100.6 cm

46
彼等に銃身を 1941
オフセット・リトグラフ
70.8×100.5 cm

60
地下鉄広告で販売促進を
リトグラフ
112.3×71.7 cm

Jean Carlu b.1900

45
America's Answer! Production
1942
Offset Lithograph 29 7/8 × 39 5/8 in
Gift of the Office for Emergency Man-
agement

46
Give 'em Both Barrels 1941
Offset Lithograph 27 7/8 × 39 1/2 in
Gift of the Office for Emergency Man-
agement

60
Stop 'em to Sell 'em 1947
Lithograph 44 1/4 × 28 1/4 in
Anonymous Gift

ウィリアム L. カークヴィル
1871—1946

13
リッピンカッツ 8月号 1895
リトグラフ
47.6×31 cm

William L. Carqueville
1871-1946

13
Lippincott's August 1895
Lithograph 18 3/4 × 12 1/4 in
Exchange

ジョン・カサド b.1944

211
ジャン・マルク 1980
シルクスクリーン
69.9×47.7 cm

John Casado b.1944

211
Jeanne Marc 1980
Silkscreen 27 1/2 × 18 3/4 in
Gift of Ivan Chermayeff

A. M. カッサンドラ 1901—1968

37
ご覧，フォードが通るよ 1937

A. M. Cassandre 1901-1968

37
Watch the Fords Go By 1937

オフセット・リトグラフ
264×594 cm

Offset Lithograph 104 × 233 7/8 in
Gift of the designer

アイヴァン・チャーマイエフ b.1932

113
目に見えぬ都市 1972
オフセット・リトグラフ
91.5×61 cm

Ivan Chermayeff b.1932

113
The lnvisible City 1972
Offset Lithograph 36 × 24 in
Gift of the designer

アイヴァン・チャーマイエフ
トーマス・ガイズマー b.1931

101
アメリカのグラフィック 1964
オフセット・リトグラフ
83.8×60.7 cm

181
パン・ナムでバリ島へ 1972
オフセット・リトグラフ
106.8×71 cm

182
パン・ナムで日本へ 1972
オフセット・リトグラフ
106.7×71 cm

185
サマー・ガーデン 1978
オフセット・リトグラフ
117×76.3 cm

206
ニューヨーク・フィルハーモニー 1978
オフセット・リトグラフ
87.7×61 cm

Ivan Chermayeff
Thomas Geismar b.1931

101
American Graphics 1964
Offset Lithograph 33 × 23 7/8 in
Exchange

181
Pan Am Bali 1972
Offset Lithograph 42 × 28 in
Gift of Pan American World Airways

182
Pan Am Japan 1972
Offset Lithograph 42 × 28 in
Gift of Pan American World Airways

185
Summergarden 1978
Offset Lithograph 46 × 30 in
Gift of the designers

206
The New York Philharmonic 1978
Offset Lithograph 34 1/2 × 24 in
Gift of the designers

アイヴァン・チャーマイエフ
トーマス・ガイズマー
ロバート・ブラウンジョン
1926—1972

Ivan Chermayeff
Thomas Geismar
Robert Brownjohn 1926-1972

112
リターン・エクシビション（3人によるグラフィックデザインの対話） 1959
オフセット・リトグラフ
70.5×55.4 cm

シーモア・クウァスト b.1931

147
ジュディ・ガーランド（コンサート） 1968
オフセット・リトグラフ
93×58.4 cm

154
臭い息を止めよ 1967
オフセット・リトグラフ
94×61 cm

192
わが芸術に歌えば 1976
シルクスクリーン
91.4×91.4 cm

186 クワスト，グレーザーの項参照

チャールズ・コイナー b.1898

48
ベストを尽くせ 1942
オフセット・リトグラフ
71.2×101.8 cm

リー・コンクリン

134
プロコール・ハラム（コンサート）
オフセット・リトグラフ
54×36 cm

143
テン・イヤーズ・アフター 1969
オフセット・リトグラフ
53.4×35.5 cm

112
A Return Exhibition 1959
Offset Lithograph 27 3/4 × 21 3/4 in
Gift of the designers

Seymour Chwast b.1931

147
Judy Garland 1968
Offset Lithograph 36 5/8 × 23 in
Gift of the designer

154
End Bad Breath 1967
Offset Lithograph 37 × 24 in
Gift of Pushpin Studios

192
With a Song in My Art 1976
Silkscreen 36 × 36 in
Gift of Pushpin, Lubalin, and Peckolick, Inc.

See also Glaser, Chwast

Charles Coiner b.1898

48
Give it Your Best！ 1942
Offset Lithograph 28 × 40 in
Gift of the Office for Emergency Management

Lee Conklin

134
Procol Harum 1969
Offset Lithograph 21 1/4 × 14 1/8 in
Gift of the designer

143
Ten Years After 1969
Offset Lithograph 21 × 14 in
Gift of the designer

コンラッド

160
畜生め 1971
シルクスクリーン
61×45.8 cm

フレデリック・ジョージ・クーパー 1892—1962

29
イギリスへのアメリカの贈物 1918
木版
75.4×51 cm

パトリック・カニンガム b.1948
ティモシー・ハースリー （写真）

184
近代建築の変遷 1979
オフセット・リトグラフ
91.5×61 cm

ルイス・ダンズィガー b.1923

96
メトロポリタン美術館所蔵アメリカ絵画展 1966
オフセット・リトグラフ
61×45.8 cm

127
ニューヨーク・スクールの第一世代展 1965
オフセット・リトグラフ
56×43.2 cm

Conrad

160
Bitch 1971
Silkscreen 24 × 18 in
Gift of the designer

Frederick George Cooper 1892-1962

29
America's Tribute to Britain 1918
Woodcut 29 5/8 × 20 in
Exchange

Patrick Cunningham b.1948
Timothy Hursley (Photograper)

184
Transformations in Modern Architecture 1979
Offset Lithograph 36 × 24 in
Commissioned by The Museum of Modern Art

Louis Danziger b.1923

96
American Paintings from The Metropolitan Museum of Art 1966
Offset Lithograph 24 × 18 in
Gift of the designer

127
New York School The First Generation 1965
Offset Lithograph 22 × 17 in
Gift of the designer

ポール・デーヴィス　b.1938

173
三文オペラ　1976
オフセット・リトグラフ
117×58.5 cm

ジム・ダイン　b.1935

163
シティー・センター　ギルバート・アンド・
サリバン　1968
オフセット・リトグラフ
89×63.5 cm

スティヴン・ドハノス　b.1907

57
不用心なお喋りの報い　1944
オフセット・リトグラフ
94.3×72.3 cm

マルセル・デュシャン　1887—1968

117
手配中　賞金2000ドル（パサデナ美術館に
おけるマルセル・デュシャン展）　1963
オフセット・リトグラフ
87.5×68.5 cm

マルセル・デュシャン
シドニー・ジャニス　b.1896

118
ダダ展　1953
オフセット・リトグラフ
96.5×63.3 cm

マイケル・エングルマン
1928—1966

Paul Davis　b.1938

173
Three Penny Opera　1976
Offset Lithograph　46 1/16 × 23 in
Gift of the New York Shakespeare Festival

Jim Dine　b.1935

163
City Center　Gilbert & Sullivan　1968
Offset Lithograph　35 × 25 in
Gift of the designer

Stevan Dohanos　b.1907

57
Award for Careless Talk　1944
Offset Lithograph　37 1/8 × 28 1/2 in
Gift of the Lauder Foundation

Marcel Duchamp　1887-1968

117
Wanted　$ 2,000 Reward　1963
Offset Lithograph　34 3/8 × 27 in
Gift of the Pasadena Art Museum

Marcel Duchamp
Sidney Janis　b.1896

118
DADA　1953
Offset Lithograph　38 × 24 7/8 in
Gift of the Sidney Janis Gallery

Michael Engelmann
1928-1966

77
お早ようはインクワイアラーから
1958
オフセット・リトグラフ
213.4×106 cm

78
お早ようはインクワイアラーから
1958
オフセット・リトグラフ
213.4×106 cm

マリソー・エスコバール　b.1930

168
パリ・レビュー　1967
シルクスクリーン
66.3×82.5 cm

ルイス・ファンチャー

26
合衆国公式戦争写真　1917
リトグラフ
104.9×71.5 cm

フェルネイゴォ

68
癌の増加　1947年頃
71.2×56 cm

ジェイムズ・モントゴメリー・フラ
ッグ　1877—1960

24
合衆国陸軍へ来れ！　1917
リトグラフ
102.2×74.4 cm

77
Good Mornings Begin with The Inquirer
1958
Offset Lithograph　84 × 41 3/4 in
Gift of the designer

78
Good Mornings Begin with The Inquirer
1958
Offset Lithograph　84 × 41 3/4 in
Gift of the designer

Marisol Escobar　b.1930

168
Paris Review　1967
Silkscreen　26 1/8 × 32 1/2 in
Gift of Page, Arbitrio and Resen

Louis Fancher

26
U. S. Official War Pictures　1917
Lithograph　41 3/8 × 28 3/16 in
Gift of the Lauder Foundation

Fellnagel

68
Cancer　c. 1947
Offset Lithograph　28 × 22 in
Gift of the designer

James Montgomery Flagg
1877-1960

24
I Want You for the U. S. Army　1917
Lithograph　40 1/4 × 29 1/4 in
Exchange

25
めざめよ アメリカ・デー　1917
リトグラフ
104.3×71.3 cm

25
Wake Up America Day　1917
Lithograph　41 1/16 × 28 1/16 in
Gift of Abby Aldrich Rockefeller

シルクスクリーン，ラッカー仕上げ
99.7×63.5 cm

Silkscreen with lacquer finish
39 1/4 × 25 in
Gift of Ivan Chermayeff

ジューリアス・フリードマン　b.1943

196
1940年代のスリラー　1980
オフセット・リトグラフ
45.8×60.9 cm

Julius Friedman　b.1943

196
Thrillers from the Forties　1980
Offset Lithograph　18 × 24 in
Gift of the designer

179
ハーマン・ミラー　サマー・ピクニック'80
1980
シルクスクリーン，ラッカー仕上げ
99.7×63.5 cm

179
Herman Miller　Summer Picnic '80
1980
Silkscreen with lacquer finish
39 1/4 × 25 in
Gift of Ivan Chermayeff

スティーヴン・フライコルム
b.1942

174
スイートコーン・フェスティバル　1970
シルクスクリーン，ラッカー仕上げ
99.7×63.5 cm

Stephen Frykholm　b.1942

174
Sweet Corn Festival　1970
Silkscreen with lacquer finish
39 1/4 × 25 in
Gift of Ivan Chermayeff

180
ミシガン州ホーランドのチューリップ
1982
シルクスクリーン，ラッカー仕上げ
63.5×100.3 cm

180
Tulip Time '82　Holland, Michigan
1982
Silkscreen with lacquer finish
25 × 39 1/2 in
Gift of the designer

175
ハーマン・ミラー　サマー・ピクニック'74
1974
シルクスクリーン，ラッカー仕上げ
99.7×63.5 cm

175
Herman Miller　Summer Picnic '74
1974
Silkscreen with lacquer finish
39 1/4 × 25 in
Gift of Ivan Chermayeff

ロバート・ゲージ　b.1921

73
レヴィーズ　ニューヨークが平らげてい
る！　1952
オフセット・リトグラフ
116.7×76.8 cm

Robert Gage　b.1921

73
Levy's　New York Is Eating It Up!
1952
Offset Lithograph　46 × 30 1/4 in
Gift of Doyle, Dane, Bernbach, Inc.

176
ハーマン・ミラー　サマー・ピクニック'75
1975
シルクスクリーン，ラッカー仕上げ
99.7×63.5 cm

176
Herman Miller　Summer Picnic '75
1975
Silkscreen with lacquer finish
39 1/4 × 25 in
Gift of Ivan Chermayeff

74
レヴィーズ　一枚食ってはまた一枚
1952
オフセット・リトグラフ，シルクスクリーン
115×75 cm

74
Levy's　One Slice Leads to Another
1952
Offset Lithograph and Silkscreen
45 1/4 × 29 1/2 in
Gift of the designer

177
ハーマン・ミラー　サマー・ピクニック'77
1977
シルクスクリーン，ラッカー仕上げ
99.7×63.5 cm

177
Herman Miller　Summer Picnic '77
1977
Silkscreen with lacquer finish
39 1/4 × 25 in
Gift of Ivan Chermayeff

ジョン A・ゲイドス

53
米大陸には敵を寄せつけない　1942
オフセット・リトグラフ
101.7×72.5 cm

John A. Gaydos

53
En Las Americas　1942
Offset Lithograph　40 × 28 1/2 in
Gift of the Office of War Information

178
ハーマン・ミラー　サマー・ピクニック'78
1978

178
Herman Miller　Summer Picnic '78
1978

ピーター・ジー　b.1932

108

ピーター・ジーのグラフィック・デザイン 1966
シルクスクリーン
51.8×42.5cm

114

ピーター・ジー殿　転居　1963
オフセット・リトグラフ
30×41.5 cm

115

ピーター・ジー殿　ウエスト・ブロードウェイ　506　1963
オフセット・リトグラフ
33.5×37.8 cm

131

株式市況　1969年頃
シルクスクリーン
78.5×53.2cm

133

ブライアント・パーク・フェスティバル 1968
シルクスクリーン
114.2×76.5cm

158

自由，平等　1968
シルクスクリーン
115.5×66 cm

159

マーチン・ルサー・キング博士　1968
シルクスクリーン
91.5×41cm

トーマス・ガイズマー
101, 206 アイヴァン・チャーマイエフの項参照

アーノルド・ゲェンス　1869—1942

30

点呼（演劇ポスター）　1918

Peter Gee　b.1932

108

Graphic Design　1966
Silkscreen　20 3/8 × 16 3/4 in
Gift of the designer

114

Peter Gee, Esq.　Not Here　1963
Offset Lithograph　11 3/4 × 16 3/8 in
Gift of the designer

115

Mr. Peter Gee　506 West Broadway
1963
Offset Lithograph　13 1/4 × 14 7/8 in
Gift of the designer

131

Market Coverage　c. 1969
Silkscreen　30 7/8 × 21 in
Gift of the designer

133

Bryant Park Festival　1968
Silkscreen　45 × 30 1/8 in
Gift of the designer

158

Freedom　Equality　1968
Silkscreen　45 1/2 × 26 in
Gift of the designer

159

Dr. Martin Luther King　1968
Silkscreen　36 × 16 1/8 in
Gift of the designer

Thomas Geismar
See Chermayeff, Geismar

Arnold Genthe　1869-1942

30

The Roll Call　1918

リトグラフ
79.4×48.2 cm

クリストス・ジャナコス　b.1934

153

青年たちを国へ還そう　1966
オフセット・リトグラフ
31×43 cm

フィリップ・ギップス　b.1931

188

エマニュエル夫人（映画）　1974
オフセット・リトグラフ
99×63.5 cm

200

スウェーデン製品　1973
オフセット・リトグラフ
75×59.8 cm

ユージン・ガイズ

31

ナジモヴァ〈サロメ〉　1922
オフセット・リトグラフ
56×70 cm

32

ナジモヴァ〈サロメ〉　1922
オフセット・リトグラフ
56×70 cm

ミルトン・グレーザー　b.1929

146

ローヴィング・スプーンフル（コンサート）
1967年頃
オフセット・リトグラフ
94.2×61 cm

Lithograph　31 1/4 × 19 in
Exchange

Christos Gianakos　b.1934

153

Send Our Boys Home　1966
Offset Lithograph　12 1/4 × 17 in
Gift of Victor Ancona and Christos
Gianakos

Philip Gips　b.1931

188

Emmanuelle　1974
Offset Lithograph　39 × 25 in
Gift of the designer

200

Imported from Sweden　1973
Offset Lithograph　29 1/2 × 23 1/2 in
Gift of the designer

Eugene Gise

31

Nazimova　Salome　1922
Offset Lithograph　22 × 27 5/8 in
Gift of the United Artists Corp.

32

Nazimova　Salome　1922
Offset Lithograph　22 × 27 5/8 in
Gift of the United Artists Corp.

Milton Glaser　b.1929

146

The Lovin' Spoonful　c. 1967
Offset Lithograph　37 1/8 × 24 in
Gift of the designer

148

ディラン　1966
オフセット・リトグラフ
83.8×55.8 cm

151

マハリア・ジャクスン（コンサート）1967
オフセット・リトグラフ
96.2×122.8 cm

152

アルバート　1976
オフセット・リトグラフ
159.5×106.7 cm

187

ビッグ・ヌード　1968
オフセット・リトグラフ
62×94.6 cm

ミルトン・グレーザー
シーモア・クウァスト

186

アンブレイカブル（プッシュピン・スタジ
オの15年展）　1971
オフセット・リトグラフ
30×124 cm

デイヴィッド・ランス・ゴーインズ
b.1945

190

嘆きの天使　1973
リトグラフ
61×42.5 cm

モートン・ゴールドショール

125

アメリカ工業デザイン協会定例会議
1968
シルクスクリーン
87×60 cm

148

Dylan　1966
Offset Lithograph　33 × 22 in
Gift of the designer

151

Mahalia Jackson　1967
Offset Lithograph　37 7/8 × 48 1/4 in
Gift of the designer

152

Albert　1976
Offset Lithograph　62 3/4 × 42 in
Gift of the designer

187

Big Nudes　1968
Offset Lithograph　24 3/8 × 37 1/4 in
Gift of the designer

Milton Glaser
Seymour Chwast

186

Unbreakable　1971
Offset Lithograph　11 7/8 × 48 7/8 in
Gift of Pushpin Studios

David Lance Goines　b.1945

190

Der Blaue Engel　1973
Lithograph　24 × 16 3/4 in
Gift of the designer and Thackrey and
Robertson

Morton Goldsholl

125

Contradictions　1968
Silkscreen　34 1/4 × 23 5/8 in
Gift of IDSA

ロイ・グレース　b. 1936

119

103回クーパー・ユニオン展覧会　1962
オフセット・リトグラフ
54.4×42 cm

ロバート・グレツコ　b.1944
チャールズ・ズィンマーマン　b.1942

121

わが街　1970（ニューヨーク都市デザイン
のための提案展）　1964
オフセット・リトグラフ
72×46.5 cm

グレン・グロー　b.1912

56

奴があなたを見張っている　1942
オフセット・リトグラフ
36×25.3 cm

ジュールス・グラン

18

スクリブナーズ　セントルイス博覧会号
1904
エッチング
57.2×37.2 cm

ケネス D. ハーク　b.1923

87

すべてのニュースを，しかも正確に　ニュ
ーヨーク・タイムズ　1951
オフセット・リトグラフ
114.2×151.7 cm

Roy Grace　b.1936

119

103 Cooper Union Exhibition　1962
Offset Lithograph　21 3/8 × 16 1/2 in
Anonymous Gift

Robert Gretczko　b.1944
Charles Zimmerman　b.1942

121

Our Town 1970　1964
Offset Lithograph　28 3/8 × 18 5/16 in
Gift of the Municipal Arts Society

Glenn Grohe　b.1912

56

He's Watching You　1942
Offset Lithograph　14 1/8 × 10 in
Gift of the Office for Emergency Man-
agement

Jules Guran

18

Scribner's　St. Louis Exposition
1904
Zinc Etching　22 5/8 × 14 5/8 in
Gift of the Lauder Foundation

Kenneth D. Haak　b.1923

87

Get All the News and Get It
Right　The New York Times　1951
Offset Lithograph　45 × 59 3/4 in
Gift of The New York Times

88
すべてのニュースを，しかも正確に　ニューヨーク・タイムズ　1951
114×151.4 cm

R. L. ハーバリィ
156 ピーター・ブラントの項参照

ルードルフ・デ・ハラク　b.1924
80
マール・マーシカーノと舞踊団　1962
オフセット・リトグラフ
43×28 cm

ルードルフ・デ・ハラク
フランク・ベネディクト　b.1951
209
ルーファス・ポーター再発見　1980
オフセット・リトグラフ
91.5×58.5 cm

ビル・ヘンリー
137
ヤングブラッヅ（ダンス・コンサート）
1968
オフセット・リトグラフ
50.5×35.6 cm

キット・ヒンリックス　b.1941
195
カリフォルニア・アメリカ・グラフィック・アーティスト協会　1982
オフセット・リトグラフ
43.2×93.3 cm

コイ・ハワード　b.1943

88
Get All the News and Get It Right
The New York Times　1951
Offset Lithograph　44 7/8 " 59 5/8 in
Gift of The New York Times

R. L. Haeberle
See Brandt, Haeberle

Rudolph de Harak　b.1924
80
Merle Marsicano　1962
Offset Lithograph　17 × 11 in
Gift of the designer

Rudolph de Harak
Frank Benedict　b.1951
209
Rufus Porter Rediscovered　1980
Offset Lithograph　36 × 23 in
Gift of the designers

Bill Henry
137
Youngbloods　1968
Offset Lithograph　19 7/8 × 14 in
Gift of the designer

Kit Hinrichs　b.1941
195
AIGA　California Design　1982
Offset Lithograph　17 × 36 3/4 in
Gift of the designer

Coy Howard　b.1943

203
コイ・ハワード〈建築とデザインに内包される多重な意味〉　1976
オフセット・リトグラフ
75.5×52.2 cm

ティモシー・ハースリー
184　パトリック・カニンガムの項参照

ロバート・インディアナ　b.1928
107
ロバート・インディアナ展（ステーブル画廊）　1962年10月16日　1962
オフセット・リトグラフ
66.3×54 cm

ノーマン・アイヴス
106
トニー・スミス　1967
シルクスクリーン
114.7×76 cm

シドニー・ジャニス
118　マルセル・デュシャンの項参照

C. H. ジョハンスン
149
ヴィジョンズ　1967
オフセット・リトグラフ
89×58.5 cm

ジャスパー・ジョーンズ　b.1930
169
ジャスパー・ジョーンズ展　2月24日―3月16日　於：レオ・カステリ画廊　1968

203
Coy Howard　Infolding of Meaning in
Architecture and Design　1976
Offset Lithograph　29 3/4 × 20 5/8 in
Gift of the designer

Timothy Hursley
See Cunningham, Hursley

Robert Indiana　b.1928
107
Indiana　Stable　16 October 62
1962
Offset Lithograph　26 1/8 × 21 1/4 in
Gift of Peter Stone

Norman Ives
106
Tony Smith　1967
Silkscreen　45 1/8 × 30 in
Gift of the designer

Sidney Janis
See Duchamp, Janis

C. H. Johansen
149
Visions　1967
Offset Lithograph　35 × 23 in
Gift of Joseph H. Heil

Jasper Johns　b.1930
169
J. Johns　24 Feb.-16 March　Leo
Castelli　1968

オフセット・リトグラフ
89.7×61 cm

カーサコヴ

69
確かめよ　梅毒防止のために血液検査を
受けよう　c. 1947
リトグラフ
71.2×56 cm

ジョエル・カッツ

123
エール映画祭　1969年頃
オフセット・リトグラフ
87.6×58.2 cm

E. ミックナイト・カウファー
1890—1954

54
枢軸側の新秩序とは……　1942
オフセット・リトグラフ
101.6×72.5 cm

ウィリアム・サージャント・ケンド
ール

16
スクリブナーズ1月号にロバート・ブラム
描く大装飾画　1900年頃
リトグラフ
43.5×31.7 cm

ラス・キニイ
183　マイケル・ボスニヤックの項参照

カール・カーラー
ヴィクター・アンコナ

Offset Lithograph　35 3/8 × 24 in
Gift of the designer

Karsakov

69
Know for Sure　Get a Blood Test
for Syphilis　c. 1947
Lithograph
28×22 in
Gift of the designer

Joel Katz

123
Yale Film Festival　c. 1969
Offset Lithograph　34 1/2 × 22 7/8 in
Gift of the designer

E. McKnight Kauffer
1890-1954

54
El Nuevo Orden　1942
Offset Lithograph　40 × 28 1/2 in
Gift of the designer

William Sargent Kendall

16
Robert Blum's Great Decorative Paint-
ing in January Scribner's　c. 1900
Lithograph　17 1/8 × 12 1/2 in
Exchange

Russ Kinne
See Bosniak, York, Kinne

Karl Koehler
Victor Ancona

55
これが敵だ　1942
オフセット・リトグラフ
86.5×61 cm

ヘンリー・カーナー

47
使った食用油を蓄えよう　1943
オフセット・リトグラフ
71×50.8 cm

58
誰かが喋った　1943年頃
オフセット・リトグラフ
87×59.7 cm

ジョージ・クリコリアン
1914—1977

89
クロスワード・パズルを毎日ニューヨー
ク・タイムズで　1950
オフセット・リトグラフ　114.3×147.3 cm

H. ランドショフ　b.1905

126
不思議の国アメリカへ行こう　1960
オフセット・リトグラフ
101×76 cm

ギルバート・レサー　b.1935

191
エクワス（劇場ドラマ）　1974
シルクスクリーン
114.3×75 cm

55
This Is the Enemy　1942
Offset Lithograph　34 × 24 in
Poster Fund

Henry Koerner

47
Save Waste Fats　1943
Offset Lithograph　28 × 20 in
Gift of the designer

58
Someone Talked　c. 1943
Offset Lithograph　34 1/4 × 23 1/2 in
Gift of the designer

George Krikorian　1914-1977

89
Crossword Puzzle　Every Day
The New York Times　1950
Offset Lithograph　45 × 58 in
Gift of The New York Times

H. Landshoff　b.1905

126
Visit Wonderland U. S. A.　1960
Offset Lithograph　39 3/4 × 30 in
Gift of the U. S. Government Printing
Office

Gilbert Lesser　b.1935

191
Equus　1974
Silkscreen　45 × 29 1/2 in
Gift of the designer

ロイ・リクテンスタイン　b.1923

170

リンカーン・センター（第4回ニューヨーク・フィルム・フェスティバル）　1966
銀紙にシルクスクリーン
116×76.2 cm

リチャード・リンドナー
1901—1978

172

アルトゥーロ・ウイの三日天下　1968
オフセット・リトグラフ
76×51 cm

リオ・リオーニ　b.1910

50

前進！　1941
オフセット・リトグラフ
97.8×73.5 cm

51

前進！　1941
オフセット・リトグラフ
101×75 cm

76

8台の自動車デザイン展　1951
オフセット・リトグラフ
25.6×66 cm

ジェイ・メーゼル
210　アーノルド・サクスの項参照

デニス・マナーキー
197　ジェフ・バーンズの項参照

Roy Lichtenstein　b.1923

170

Lincoln Center　1966
Silkscreen on silver paper
45 3/4 ×30 in
Gift of the designer

Richard Lindner　1901-1978

172

The Resistable Rise of Arturo Ui
1968
Offset Lithograph
29 15/16 × 20 1/16 in
Gift of Peter Stone

Leo Lionni　b.1910

50

Keep 'em Rolling!　1941
Offset Lithograph　38 1/2 × 29 in
Gift of the Office for Emergency Management

51

Keep 'em Rolling!　1941
Offset Lithograph　39 3/4 × 29 1/2 in
Gift fo the Office for Emergency Management

76

8 Automobies　1951
Offset Lithograph　10 × 26 in
Commissioned by The Museum of Modern Art

Jay Maisel
See Saks, Scharrenbroich, Maisel

Dennis Manarchy
See Barnes, Manarchy

ヘンリー・マーコウィッツ
95　ロバート・ブランドワインの項参照

ハーバート・マター　b.1907

52

アメリカが呼んでいる　1941
オフセット・リトグラフ
102.5×75 cm

72

この子等のうちの一人は小児麻痺に罹った　1950
オフセット・リトグラフ
116×74 cm

79

単脚椅子　1957年頃
オフセット・リトグラフ
114.2×66 cm

81

ジャコメッティ展　1966
オフセット・リトグラフ
127×90 cm

ピーター・マックス　b.1937

142

キャプテン・ミッドナイト第12号　1966
オフセット・リトグラフ
91.5×61 cm

ジョン・ミクヴィッカー

122

アトミズムとフォルム　1965
オフセット・リトグラフ
61×45.8 cm

199

あの興奮が戻って来る　1970年頃
オフセット・リトグラフ

Henry Markowitz
See Brandwein, Markowitz

Herbert Matter　b.1907

52

America Calling　1941
Offset Lithograph　40 3/8 × 29 1/2 in
Gift of the Office for Emergency Management

72

One of Them Had Polio　1950
Offset Lithograph　45 3/4 × 29 1/8 in
Gift of the Infantile Paralysis Foundation

79

Single Pedestal Furniture　c. 1957
Offset Lithograph　45 × 26 in
Gift of the designer

81

Giacometti　1966
Offset Lithograph　50 × 35 1/2 in
Gift of the designer

Peter Max　b.1937

142

#12　Captain Midnight　1966
Offset Lithograph　36 × 24 in
Gift of the East Hampton Gallery, N. Y.

John McVicker

122

Atomism and Form　1965
Offset Lithograph　24 × 18 in
Gift of the School of Visual Arts

199

The Thrill Is Back　c. 1970
Offset Lithograph　45 × 59 1/2 in

114.5×151 cm

Gift of the New York Racing Association

ジョン・ミクヴィッカー
ボブ・パイク（写真）

198
ビッグ A（競馬）10月28日-12月10日
1970
オフセット・リトグラフ
91.5×114.5 cm

ハーバート・ミグドール　b.1935

120
フォトグラフィック・ポスター　　1964
写真印画紙，インク補彩
140.5×69 cm

ジェームズ・ミホ　b.1931

102
ミホ（個展ポスター）　　1972
オフセット・リトグラフ
69.8×47.7 cm

トモコ・ミホ　b.1931

128
シカゴの大建築　　1967
シルクスクリーン，アルミ箔紙
126×88.5 cm

129
ニューヨークへの65の橋　　1968
オフセット・リトグラフ，シルクスクリー
ン
114.3×75 cm

John McVicker
Bob Pike (Photographer)

198
Big A　　Oct. 28-Dec. 10　　1970
Offset Lithograph　36 ×45 in
Gift of Jack Banning

Herbert Migdoll　b.1935

120
The Photographic Poster　　1964
Photo blowup with yellow ink
55 3/8 × 27 1/8 in
Commissioned by The Museum of Modern Art

James Miho　b.1931

102
Miho　　1972
Offset Lithograph　27 1/2 × 18 3/4 in
Gift of the designer

Tomoko Miho　b.1931

128
Great Architecture in Chicago　　1967
Silkscreen on aluminized paper
49 5/8 × 34 7/8 in
Gift of the Container Corporation of America

129
65 Bridges to New York　　1968
Offset Lithograph and Silkscreen
45 × 29 1/2 in
Gift of the designer

ロバート・モンドロック
157　ハワード・ブリュームの項参照

ヴィクター・モスコソ　b.1936

135
ブルー・チアー（ダンスコンサート）1967
オフセット・リトグラフ
51×35.6 cm

136
クイックシルバー・メッセンジャー・サー
ヴィス　　1967
オフセット・リトグラフ
51.5×35.5 cm

138
ジュニア・ウエルズ（コンサート）　　1966
オフセット・リトグラフ
50.5×35.5 cm

144
リーヴァイスで寛ごう　　1967年頃
オフセット・リトグラフ
78.8×61 cm

ヴィクター・モスコソ
ポール・ユーバック（写真）

139
オーティス・ラッシュ（コンサート）　1967
オフセット・リトグラフ
50.8×35.7 cm

スタンリー・マウス

141
マザーズ・オヴ・インヴェンション　1967
オフセット・リトグラフ
55.5×32.3 cm

Robert Mondlock
See Blume, Borowski, Mondlock

Victor Moscoso　b.1936

135
Blue Cheer　　1967
Offset Lithograph　20 × 14 in
Gift of the designer

136
Quicksilver Messenger Service　　1967
Offset Lithograph　20 1/4 × 14 in
Gift of the designer

138
Junior Wells　　1966
Offset Lithograph　19 7/8 × 14 in
Gift of the designer

144
Rest in Levi's　　c. 1967
Offset Lithograph　31 × 24 in
Gift of the designer

Victor Moscoso
Paul Ubac (Photographer)

139
Otis Rush　　1967
Offset Lithograph　20 × 14 in
Gift of the designers

Stanley Mouse

141
Mothers of Invention　　1967
Offset Lithograph　21 3/4 × 12 5/8 in
Gift of the designer

エリック・ニッチ　b.1908

61
迅速，反復，あざやかに　1947
リトグラフ
111.7×71 cm

82
ジェネラル・ダイナミックス　宇宙への第一歩　1955年頃
リトグラフ
127.5×89 cm

83
ジェネラル・ダイナミックス　流体力学　1955
リトグラフ
127.5×90 cm

84
ジェネラル・ダイナミックス　核融合　1958
リトグラフ
127.5×90 cm

85
ジェネラル・アトミック　訓練研究原子炉　1958
オフセット・リトグラフ
128×90 cm

ジョン・ナンマン　b. 1936

109
ポピュラー視覚芸術祭　1965
シルクスクリーン
65.6×44.8 cm

ジョン・ウォーナー・ノートン
1876―1934

21
奴らをアメリカに寄せつけるな

Erik Nitsche　b.1908

61
Say It Fast　Often　in Color　1947
Lithograph　44 × 28 in
Gift of the designer

82
General Dynamics　First Step into Space　c. 1955
Lithograph　50 1/4 × 35 in
Anonymous Gift

83
General Dynamics　Hydrodynamics 1955
Lithograph　50 1/4 × 35 3/8 in
Gift of the General Dynamics Corporation

84
General Dynamics　Nuclear Fusion 1958
Lithograph　50 1/4 × 35 3/8 in
Gift of the General Dynamics Corporation

85
General Atomic　Triga　1958
Offset Lithograph　50 3/8 × 35 3/8 in
Exchange

John Noneman　b.1936

109
Popular Optical Artball　1965
Silkscreen　25 7/8 × 17 5/8 in
Gift of the designer

John Warner Norton
1876-1934

21
Keep These Off the U.S.A.　1918

リトグラフ
102×77 cm

マックスフィールド・パリッシュ
1870―1966

17
スクリブナーズ　1897
リトグラフ
50.5×36.2 cm

エドワード・ペンフィールド
1866―1925

9
ハーパーズ　3月号　1897
エッチング
35.6×48.5 cm

10
ハーパーズ　3月号　1895
エッチング
49×35 cm

11
ハーパーズ　7月号　1894
エッチング
45.8×31.7 cm

12
ハーパーズ　8月号　1896
エッチング
47.2×34.3 cm

ジョセフ・ペネル　1860―1926

23
この自由は滅びない　1917年頃
リトグラフ
103×73.8 cm

コールズ・フィリップス

Lithograph　40 1/8 × 30 1/4 in
Exchange

Maxfield Parrish　1870-1966

17
Scribner's　1897
Lithograph　19 7/8 × 14 1/4 in
Anonymous Gift

Edward Penfield　1866-1925

9
Harper's　March　1897
Zinc Etching　14 × 19 1/16 in
Gift of Poster Originals

10
Harper's　March　1895
Zinc Etching　19 1/4 × 13 3/4 in
Exchange

11
Harper's　July　1894
Zinc Etching　18 × 12 1/2 in
Exchange

12
Harper's　August　1896
Zinc Etching　18 9/16 × 13 9/16 in
Exchange

Joseph Pennell　1860-1926

23
That Liberty Shall Not Perish
c. 1917
Lithograph　40 1/2 × 29 in
Gift of John D. Rockefeller III

Coles Phillips

28
明りが石炭を食う　1917年頃
リトグラフ
71×52 cm

ボブ・パイク
198　ジョン・ミクヴィッカーの項参照

ポール・ランド　b.1914
62
地下鉄ポスターはうける　1947
オフセット・リトグラフ
115×74.5 cm

63
インターフェイス・デー　1951
シルクスクリーン
114×76.5 cm

64
インターフェイス・デー　1954
オフセット・リトグラフ
114.2×74 cm

99
20世紀デザインの源泉と現状　1966
オフセット・リトグラフ
61×70.5 cm

100
IBM　1982
オフセット・リトグラフ
91.5×61 cm

ロバート・ラウシェンバーグ
b.1925
202
レオ・カスティリ画廊でのロバート・ラウ
シェンバーグ展　1980
オフセット・リトグラフ
78×56.3 cm

28
Light Consumes Coal　　c. 1917
Lithograph　28 × 21 1/2 in
Exchange

Bob Pike
See McVicker, Pike

Paul Rand　b. 1914
62
Subway Posters Score　1947
Offset Lithograph　45 1/4 × 29 3/8 in
Gift of the designer

63
Interfaith Day　1951
Silkscreen　44 7/8 × 30 1/8 in
Gift of the designer

64
Interfaith Day　1954
Offset Lithograph　45 × 29 1/8 in
Gift of the designer

99
Sources and Resources　1966
Offset Lithograph　21 × 27 3/4 in
Gift of the designer

100
IBM　1982
Offset Lithograph　36 × 24 in
Gift of the designer

Robert Rauschenberg　b.1925
202
R. R. at Leo's　1980
Offset Lithograph　30 3/4 × 22 1/8 in
Gift of the Leo Castelli Gallery

マン・レイ　1890—1976
35
地下鉄がロンドンを動かす　1932
オフセット・リトグラフ
101×62 cm

ジョン・リーベン　b.1935
103
シカゴ　ファン・デル・ローエたちの建て
た街　1966
シルクスクリーン
127×89 cm

104
ディアボーン天文台　1966
シルクスクリーン
126.8×89 cm

ラリー・リバーズ　b.1923
162
第1回ニューヨーク映画祭　1963
リトグラフ
115×76.2 cm

ロバート・マイルズ・ランヤン
b.1925
161
第17回アスペン国際デザイン会議
1967
オフセット・リトグラフ
93.7×62 cm

エドワード・ルーシャ　b.1937
145
メード・イン・カリフォルニア　1971
オフセット・リトグラフ
94×58.5 cm

Man Ray　1890-1976
35
Keeps London Going　1932
Offset Lithograph　39 3/4 × 24 3/8 in
Gift of Bernard Davis

John Rieben　b.1935
103
Chicago The Town that Van der Rohe
Built　1966
Silkscreen　50 × 35 in
Gift of the Container Corporation of
America

104
Dearborn Observatory　1966
Silkscreen　49 7/8 × 35 in
Gift of the Container Corporation of
America

Larry Rivers　b.1923
162
First New York Film Festival　1963
Lithograph　45 1/4 × 30 in
Gift of Lincoln Center, N. Y.

Robert Miles Runyan　b.1925

161
17th International Design Conference in
Aspen　1967
Offset Lithograph　36 7/8 × 24 3/8 in
Gift of the designer

Edward Ruscha　b.1937
145
Made in California　1971
Offset Lithograph　37 ×23 in
Exchange

ジョージ・セデック　b.1928

208

イタリアのアイディア　　1981
オフセット・リトグラフ
96.5×61 cm

アーノルド・サクス　b.1931
インゴ・シャーレンブロイク
b. 1937
ジェイ・メーゼル（写真）

210

オーティスの世界　　1981
オフセット・リトグラフ
66×91.5 cm

インゴ・シャーレンブロイク
210　アーノルド・サクスの項参照

ジョー・スコーソニィ　b.1942

205

スポット・ラン　スポット・ラン（映画）
1974
オフセット・リトグラフ
40×60 cm

ベン・シャーン　1898—1969

65

反動の支配を打ち破れ　　1944
シルクスクリーン
105.7×73.8 cm

111

バレエ　U. S. A.　　1959
シルクスクリーン
79.8×54.2 cm

テッド・シェイン

George Sadek　b.1928

208

The Italian Idea　　1981
Offset Lithograph　38 × 24 in
Gift of the designer

Arnold Saks　b.1931
Ingo Scharrenbroich　b.1937
Jay Maisel (Photographer)

210

The World of Otis　　1981
Offset Lithograph　26 × 36 in
Gift of the designers

Ingo Scharrenbroich
See Saks, Scharrenbroich, Maisel

Joe Scorsone　b.1942

205

Spot Run Spot Run　　1974
Offset Lithograph　15 3/4 × 23 5/8 in
Gift of the designer

Ben Shahn　1898-1969

65

Break Reaction's Grip　　1944
Offset Lithograph　41 5/8 × 29 in
Gift of S. S. Spivack

111

Ballets U. S. A.　　1959
Silkscreen　31 3/8 × 21 3/8 in
Anonymous Gift

Ted Shaine

140

ターン・オン，チューン・イン，ドロップ・
アウト　　1967
シルクスクリーン
71.5×50.7 cm

オーティス・シェパード　b.1894

36

リグレイのスペアミント・ガム　　1936
リトグラフ
106.8×71.1 cm

ルイス・シルバー・スタイン

86

WQXR　　1955
オフセット・リトグラフ
113.6×76.2 cm

J. アレン・セント・ジョン

20

ドイツ野郎の痕跡を消し去れ　　1917
オフセット・リトグラフ
105.5×68.5 cm

ソール・スタインバーグ　b.1914

165

ドローイング，その他（個展ポスター）
1952
写真印画紙，インク補彩
72×57 cm

166

マーグ・ファンデーションの夕べ　　1970
オフセット・リトグラフ
89×57.5 cm

140

Turn On　　Tune In　　Drop Out
1967
Silkscreen　28 1/4 × 20 in
Gift of Joseph H. Heil

Otis Shepherd　b.1894

36

Wrigley's Spearmint Gum　　1936
Lithograph　42 × 28 in
Gift of the Wrigley Co.

Louis Silverstein

86

WQXR　　1955
Offset Lithograph　44 3/4 × 30 in
Gift of The New York Times

J. Allen St. John

20

The Hun　　His Mark　　Blot It Out
1917
Offset Lithograph　41 1/2 × 27 in
Exchange

Saul Steinberg　b.1914

165

Drawings, Etc.　　1952
Photo blowup with ink notations
28 5/16 × 22 7/16 in
Gift of the Intstitute of Contemporary
Art

166

Nuits de la Foundation Maeght　　1970
Offset Lithograph　35 × 22 5/8 in
Gift of Peter Stone

167
スポレト・フェスティバル　1969
オフセット・リトグラフ
102×76.2 cm

フランク・ステラ　b.1936

171
リンカーン・センター・フェスティバル'67
1967
オフセット・リトグラフ
114.2×75 cm

ピーター・テューブナー

130
ハーレム　1968
オフセット・リトグラフ
114.4×75 cm

マルク・トゥライブ　b.1943

212
アドルフ・ロス　1978
ジアゾ・プリント
61×45.6 cm

213
日本建築の新しい波　1978
ジアゾ・プリント
61×229.8 cm

ジョージ・チャーニー　b.1924

97
スクール・オブ・ヴィジュアル・アート 1959
オフセット・リトグラフ
116.8×76.2 cm

98
すべての壁は扉である　1961
オフセット・リトグラフ
116.8×76.2 cm

167
Spoleto Festival　1969
Offset Lithograph　40 1/4 × 30 in
Gift of Peter Stone

Frank Stella　b.1936

171
Lincoln Center Festival '67　1967
Offset Lithograph　45 × 29 1/2 in
Gift of List Art Posters

Peter Teubner

130
Harlem　1968
Offset Lithograph　45 × 29 1/2 in
Gift of the designer

Marc Treib　b.1934

212
Adolph Loos　1978
Diazo Print　24 × 18 in
Gift of the designer

213
New Wave of Japanese Architecture
1978
Diazo Print　24 × 90 1/2 in
Gift of the designer

George Tscherny　b.1924

97
School of Visual Arts　1959
Offset Lithograph　46 × 30 in
Gift of the designer

98
Every Wall Is a Door　1961
Offset Lithograph　46 × 30 in
Gift of the designer

207
19世紀のドイツ　1981
オフセット・リトグラフ
73.7×55.2 cm

ポール・ユーバック
139　ヴィクター・モスコソの項参照

作者不明

1
ウォルター L. メイン　三つのリング・ショー　1900年頃
リトグラフ
71.6×106.4 cm

8
ヴィクター自転車　1898年頃
リトグラフ
72.5×49.8 cm

14
J. マンツ・アンド・カンパニー　1896年頃
リトグラフ
47.2×29.7 cm

19
勝利のために公債を　1917年頃
オフセット・リトグラフ
74.2×48.7 cm

44
降下海兵隊　1941
オフセット・リトグラフ
152.5×98.5 cm

49
増産を　1942年頃
オフセット・リトグラフ
101.7×72.4 cm

207
Germany in the 19th Century　1981
Offset Lithograph　29 × 21 in
Gift of the designer

Paul Ubak
See **Moscoso, Ubak**

Unknown

1
Walter L. Main　3 Ring Shows
c. 1895
Lithograph　28 1/4 × 41 7/8 in
Anonymous Gift

8
Victor Cycles　c. 1898
Lithograph　28 1/2 × 19 5/8 in
Gift of the Lauder Foundation

14
J. Manz & Co.　c. 1896
Lithograph　18 9/16 × 11 11/16 in
Exchange

19
V　Invest　c. 1917
Offset Lithograph　29 1/4 × 19 1/8 in
Gift of John D. Rockefeller III

44
Paramarines　1941
Offset Lithograph　60 × 38 3/4 in
Anonymous Gift

49
More Production　1942
Offset Lithograph　40 × 28 1/2 in
Gift of the War Production Board

155
こいつは東南アジア向けの本物だ
1970年頃
シルクスクリーン
38×28 cm

アンディ・ウォーホール　b.1930

116
パリ・レヴュー　　1968
シルクスクリーン
94×68.7 cm

132
第5回ニューヨーク映画祭　リンカーン・
センター　1967
シルクスクリーン
114.3×61 cm

ウエストマコット

105
オーケストラ・ホール　　1966
シルクスクリーン
127×89 cm

デニス・ウィラー　b.1935

92
まず〈ライフ〉を開こう　　1963年頃
シルクスクリーン
116×151 cm

93
スカイラインに届け〈ライフ〉　　1963
シルクスクリーン
116×151 cm

チャールズ・ホワイト三世

155
It's the Real Thing for S. E. Asia
c. 1970
Silkscreen　15 × 11 in
Anonymous Gift

Andy Warhol　b.1930

116
Paris Review　　1968
Silkscreen　37 × 27 in
Gift of Page, Arbitrio and Resen

132
Film Festival　Lincoln Center　　1967
Silkscreen　45 × 24 in
Peter Stone Poster Fund

Westmacott

105
Orchestra Hall　　1966
Silkscreen　50 × 35 in
Gift of the Container Corporation of
America

Dennis Wheeler　b.1935

92
Any Way You Slice It　　Life
c. 1963
Silkscreen　45 5/8 × 59 1/2 in
Gift of Time Life, Inc.

93
Reach for the Skyline　　Life　　1963
Silkscreen　45 5/8 × 59 1/2 in
Gift of Time Life, Inc.

Charles White III

194
ご来場の皆さん　ローリング・ストーンズ
です　1974
オフセット・リトグラフ
34.9×99 cm

デイヴィッド・ウィルコックス

150
ニーナ・シモーヌ　　1970
オフセット・リトグラフ
70.2×48.4 cm

チャールズ・ハーバート・ウッドベ
リー　1864—1940

15
センチュリー　7月号　　1895
エッチング
48×29.8 cm

ランス・ワイマン
ビル・キャナン

124
スタジアム　1972
オフセット・リトグラフ
87.8×61 cm

ハワード・ヨーク

183　マイケル・ボスニヤックの項参照

エルスウォース・ヤング

22
ベルギーを忘れるな　　1918
リトグラフ
76.5×50.5 cm

194
Ladies and Gentlemen　　The Rolling
Stones　1974
Offset Lithograph　13 3/4 × 39 in
Gift of the designer

David Wilcox

150
Nina Simone　　1970
Offset Lithograph　27 5/8 × 19 in
Gift of the designer

Charles Herbert Woodbury
1864-1940

15
The July Century　　1895
Zinc Etching　18 7/8 × 11 3/4 in
Exchange

Lance Wyman
Bill Cannan

124
Stadium　1972
Offset Lithograph　34 5/8 × 24 in
Gift of the designer

Howard York
See Bosniak, York, Kinne

Ellsworth Young

22
Remember Belgium　　1918
Lithograph　30 1/8 × 19 7/8 in
Exchange

チャールズ・ズィンマーマン　　Charles Zimmerman
121　ロバート・グレツコの項参照　*See* **Gretczko, Zimmerman**

謝辞

　ニューヨーク近代美術館のグラフィック・デザインのコレクションには数千点にのぼるポスターが収蔵されているが，これは規模の点でも他の分野のコレクション同様，国際的なものである。今回展観され，カタログに掲載されるポスターは，その一部分に過ぎない。しかも，ほとんど一世紀にわたって製作されたにもかかわらず，これらアメリカのポスターはその理念において近代的なのである。

　ポスターを選ぶために多くの資料を撰り分けたり，記録を調べたり，最終的に出品の決まったポスターを撮影したりする仕事は厖大なものであった。美術館内外の非常に多くの人が，さまざまの方法で協力してくれたが，特に以下の人々の協力は特筆すべきものであった。この展覧会計画全体に関して貴重な協力をしてくれたロバート・コーツ，アントニエット・キングの下で補修を必要とするポスターの修理を担当してくれたイヴリン・コーンライン，調査を助け，全資料をタイプしてくれたヴィクトリア・ケンドール，また，このカタログに掲載されたカラーの全写真及びモノクローム写真の大部分を撮影してくれたジェイムズ・ウェリング等である。事実，次の番号の作品以外はすべて彼が撮影したものである。（撮影・ケート・ケラーおよびマリ・オラタンジ：89，94，173；ジェイムズ・マシューズ：44，74，109，118，128，149，183；ロルフ・ピータースン：93；ソーイチ・スナミ：35，39，46，58，59，63，76；オリバー・ベーカー：145）

　最後に，私が本展を企画しこの本を製作するにあたり，助言を与えていただいた京都国立近代美術館学芸課長 内山武夫氏と同館のスタッフの全面的な協力に対し，心から感謝の意を表するものである。

ニューヨーク近代美術館　建築・デザイン部
J. ステュワート・ジョンソン

Acknowledgements

The Museum of Modern Art's collection of graphic design contains thousands of posters and like all of the Museum's collections is international in scope. This catalogue and exhibition concentrate on just one segment of it: American posters, which, though designed over a period of almost a century in time, are modern in their conception.

The tasks of sifting quantities of material in order to make choices, of documentation, of making photographs of the posters finally selected for inclusion, were formidable. Numerous people both within the Museum and on the outside helped in many ways but several deserve special mention. They are Robert Coates, whose work on all aspects of the project was invaluable; Evelyn Koehnline, who under the supervision of Antoinette King treated all those posters requiring conservation; Victoria Kendall, who latterly aided with research and did all of the typing; and James Welling, who took all of the color transparencies and the great majority of black-and-white photographs published here. In fact all photographs are by him, with the following exceptions: 89, 94, and 173 by Kate Keller and Mali Olatunji; 44, 74, 109, 118, 128, 149 and 183 by James Mathews; 93 by Rolf Petersen; 35, 39, 46, 58, 59, 63, and 76 by Soichi Sunami; and 145 by Oliver Baker.

Finally, I should like to thank Takeo Uchiyama, Chief Curator of The National Museum of Modern Art, Kyoto, who suggested to me this exhibition and book, and his staff all the work they have devoted to the project.

J. Stewart Johnson
Curator: Department of Architecture and Design
The Museum of Modern Art, New York

ニューヨーク近代美術館所蔵品による20世紀アメリカのポスター

編集・発行　京都国立近代美術館・ニューヨーク近代美術館
印　　刷　日本写真印刷株式会社
Ⓒ１９８３　京都国立近代美術館・ニューヨーク近代美術館